When I read Frances Vaughan's fir[...] ized I had found a fellow incarnat[...] such as inspiration, insight, imag[...] I find to my delight that the disca[...] taking part in a cross–world channeling project, collaborating with the incarnate spirit of Cynthia Spring.

Frances has now joined the ranks of those myriad discarnate sources who comprise the channeled literature that I have been consuming all these years. Now all you fellow readers can share in this larger reality. Our human consensus reality here on earth is increasingly awakening to a shared understanding of the true interactive nature of the larger reality. I am excited to be among all the incarnate and discarnate spirits who know this larger truth with love at its very core. Thank you, Frances and Cynthia, for what you have given us.

> JON KLIMO, PH.D., Author, *Channeling: Investigations on Receiving Information from Paranormal Sources*; Co-author (with Pamela Heath. M.D.), *Handbook to the Afterlife*

In 1931, revolutionary quantum physicist and Nobel Prize winner Max Planck said, "I regard consciousness as fundamental . . . everything we talk about, everything we regard as existing, postulates consciousness." Given this idea that the basic make-up of the universe is consciousness, it is not surprising that Cynthia Spring and Frances Vaughan are in contact beyond the veil of death. The information contained in their conversations is provocative, inspiring, and practical. They brilliantly include ways in which we, too, can contact those who exist on the non-material plane with questions of our own. I recommend both this book and Book One, and look forward to the third book in the trilogy.

> JUSTINE WILLIS TOMS, Co-founder, Director, Host of New Dimensions Radio; Author, *Small Pleasures: Finding Grace in a Chaotic World*

What a delightful, well-written, how-to manual for those with questions, concerns and wonderings about our world and all the other elements of our spiritual environment. This *Seven Questions* book takes the reader through a step-by step understanding of consciousness, its construction, and methods by which readers can experience their own expansion and awareness of life. I find the questions from Cynthia to be deep and far-reaching, enabling the answers from Frances to be on point in her guidance and perceptions. Blessings to you and Frances for providing this knowledge for those who are ready to know more.

JEANNE LOVE, Medium, Channel and Spiritual Teacher

This book offers a threshold into an expanded consciousness. It is a thought-provoking dialogue between Frances Vaughan and Cynthia Spring that explains the origins of the current upheavals of our world. It also offers profound counsel into how we can maintain our balance and our moral values during this collective crisis. Beyond that, it presents a simple, 7-step process for a direct experience of communication with a loved one "on the other side." All of that packed into one small book. What a treasure!

LISA SMARTT, Author, *Words at the Threshold, Veil,* and *Cante Bardo;* Founder, The Final Words Project.

Seven Questions

About The Greater Reality

BOOK TWO
of the *Greater Reality* Series

Cynthia Spring and Frances Vaughan

Wisdom Circles Publishing

Seven Questions about The Greater Reality: Book Two by Cynthia Spring
and Frances Vaughan. Copyright © 2020 by Cynthia Spring.
All rights reserved.

Wisdom Circles Publishing
1063 Leneve Place
El Cerrito, CA 94530
www.cindyspring.com
wave@cindyspring.com

For complete list of permissions for quoted material, please see
"Permissions" (p. 171)

Cover graphic: kevron2002/*depositphotos.com*

Typesetting and Design: Margaret Copeland, Terragrafix
www.terragrafix.com

Publishing Consultant: Naomi Rose
www.naomirose.net

Proofreading: Gabriel Steinfeld
gstein@sonic.net

Author photograph: Stu Selland

BISAC: SEL032000
SELF-HELP / Spiritual

Printed in the United States of America
First printing 2020

ISBN # 978-0-9996989-3-8

Dedicated to all those who want to co-create new ways of being from a place of courage, wonder and love.

~◎

I asked Frances at one point in our sessions for *Book Two* if those of us living today could possibly imagine the inhabitants and forms of the world to come. She answered: *"Could the dinosaurs imagine skyscrapers? I don't think so."*

Contents

To Our Dear Readers

Welcome to *Book Two* of the *Greater Reality* Series. Here we'll consider how to maintain our balance, our equilibrium as individual incarnate souls, within an increasingly chaotic and fear-filled world. *Book Two* continues the work of *Book One* that Frances Vaughan and I began in January of 2018 through automatic writing, also known as channeling. She had passed on in the fall of 2017. This became a collaboration between two souls, one incarnate on earth and one on the other side, who share a greater reality.

I invite you to join us again in the expanding consciousness that Frances has introduced to me. For me, this has been *direct experience*. I am waking up to my next stage of development in this human life — recognition of a greater reality. The same evolutionary thrust that has moved me through the stages of my life now has revealed that there is yet more to be: a participant in a Consciousness that includes all — everyone, everything, within a greater Whole — and unites all with the Source. My desire is to know and experience the greater reality while still incarnate — to know the physical and the nonphysical — and to recognize they are One within an infinite Ocean of Love. Frances has helped me to see a greater reality permeated with Divine Light, populated by innumerable souls in communion within a much larger frame than the space/time dimension. The subtitle of this book puts it all succinctly: ***We are spiritual beings having a human experience.*** We are embarking on an exploration of that truth — you and I, with Frances Vaughan as our guide. So let's begin.

INTRODUCTION

This book is about a consciousness that is evolving, unfolding, and in which we're all participating — collaboratively and creatively as unique individuals. It's part magic carpet ride, and it's part labor-intensive demolition of the hypnotic programming of materialism we've all inherited.

— From *Seven Questions about Life After Life*, Book One
of the *Greater Reality* Series

The primary learning from *Book One* was: death is a transition to another form of existence. The first volume also explored what is often called "a greater reality," and offered portals for the reader to have a more direct experience than simply reading words on a page. Also, Frances mentioned "upcoming upheavals." We are going through a tumultuous time of rebalance and greater vision. Such times always involve destruction and letting go of old forms. It will help if we remember:

- We exist in a greater reality than simply within our earth incarnation.
- This is only one lifetime among many.
- There is no One Reality we must adhere to. There are many realities.
- We are bonded forever to those we love and who love us.

We are in the midst of a mind shift more grand than the one that began in the 16th century. That was when we began to find out, much to our dismay, that the Earth was not the center of the universe. Copernicus proved by using math, and then Galileo by using a telescope, that in fact, the Earth is rather a small player in the cosmic scheme of things.

Now we are finding out that the human body, precious and amazing as it is, is not the center of the *individual's* universe. The physical form is an expression of our much more expansive consciousness. So what has allowed us to break free from the limited space/time perception to a much broader sense of our participation in the nonmaterial world?

A Shift in Consciousness

In the mid-19th century, the standard explanation from the world of science was that The Big Bang produced a lot of lifeless matter, which in time produced living matter that — through twists of evolution — resulted in higher forms. Those forms eventually led to the consciousness of human beings. This Darwinian description became dogma — that is, truth not to be questioned. But in the last half of the 19th century, the dogma began to show cracks that let in more light. In fact, it was the study of the nature of light where the breakthroughs happened. This became known as quantum physics. Why were these discoveries so "earth-shattering?" Willis Harman, professor of engineering and long-time president of the Institute of Noetic Sciences, founded by astronaut Edgar Mitchell, put it this way in his book, *Higher Creativity*:

> In the alternative picture of evolution that is beginning to emerge from quantum physics, we find that rather than consciousness evolving from the universe, the universe evolved from consciousness, and that consciousness seems to have "pulled" the evolutionary process in certain preferred directions.

Since the mid-20th century, the study of consciousness has become a gold mine for exploration and untapped human potentials. How do we explain the well-documented abilities of some people to send messages to other people at a distance (telepathy)? Or to send their minds to distant countries and describe what they see there (remote viewing)? Or to predict a disaster before it happens (precognition)? Each of these abilities points to a human capacity that goes far beyond the boundaries of the physical body.

More evidence began pouring in during the 1960s with detailed reports from dedicated researchers who studied people who had had near-death experiences (Raymond Moody), or out-of-body experiences, (Robert Monroe), or children who could recall past lives with verifiable details (Ian Stevenson). (See *References*)

We are waking up to the awareness that we are more than our bodies. In fact, we exist beyond our temporal lifetimes as members of nonphysical realities. Systems scientist and philosopher Ervin Laszlo strongly supports this finding in his book, *The Intelligence of the Cosmos: Why Are We Here? New Answers from the Frontiers of Science*:

> *Are we a body that generates the stream of sensations we call consciousness, or are we a consciousness associated with a body that displays it? Do we have consciousness, or are we consciousness?*

Another popular way of explaining this concept is to use the analogy of a radio or TV. Does the box contain all those people talking and musicians playing? No. The radio or TV is the *medium*, not the creator of the sounds. So too is our brain the processor of consciousness. When the radio is turned off, the sounds continue to exist. As Laszlo puts it:

Just like the program broadcast over the air continues to exist when my TV set is turned off, my consciousness continues to exist when my brain is turned off. Consciousness is a real element in the real world. The brain and body do not produce it; they display it. And it does not cease when life in the body does.

The Shift in Western Religion

In the mid-18th century, western religion began grappling with whether the body has a soul, or whether one way the soul expressed itself was in a physical form. The person most often cited as initiating this discussion was Christian mystic and philosopher Emanuel Swedenborg, who wrote:

*When someone's body can no longer perform its functions in the natural world in response to the thoughts and affections of its spirit (which it derives from the spiritual world), then we say that the individual has died. This happens when the lungs' breathing and the heart's systolic motion have ceased. The person, though, has not died at all. We are only separated from the physical nature that was useful to us in the world. The essential person is actually still alive. I say that the essential person is still alive because **we are not people because of our bodies but because of our spirits.** After all, it is the spirit within us that thinks, and thought and affection together make us the people we are. We can see, then, that when we die we simply move from one world into another.*

The Eastern philosophies of Hinduism and Buddhism had already posited, for over two millennia, the impermanence of the body and a being's existence through many lifetimes. American spiritual teacher Ram Dass, who embraced a Hindu path called *bhakti yoga*, put it this way:

> *These bodies we live in, and the ego that identifies with it, are just like the old family car. They are functional entities in which our Soul travels through our incarnation. But when they are used up, they die. The most graceful thing to do is to just allow them to die peacefully and naturally — to "let go lightly." Through it all, who we are is Soul . . . and when the body and the ego are gone, the Soul will live on, because the Soul is eternal. Eventually, in some incarnation, when we've finished our work, our Soul can merge back into the One . . . back into God . . . back into the Infinite. In the meantime, our Soul is using bodies, egos, and personalities to work through the karma of each incarnation.*

These messages, from both science and religion, are pointing at the same understanding: Consciousness is the primary stuff of the universe as we know it, and our physical existence is one form of expression, an incarnation of that consciousness. Put simply: you do not *have* a soul, you *are* an eternal soul. You *have* a body that is temporal — that is, subject to space/time limitations, including death. This shift in awareness — about being a soul that has a body — is the central theme of *Book Two*. That understanding is an enormous shift for nearly all of us.

In *Book Two*, Frances continues to give us glimpses of "the other side," continues to put larger frames on current events, and offers suggestions on how to navigate the scary and the painful in a time of upheavals of all kinds. We will also continue to stress the importance of having direct experience of the greater reality.

In *Book One,* we suggested several dozen portals for entry. In *Book Two,* we will concentrate on developing just one portal: that of automatic writing, or channeling. You will be gently encouraged to try your hand at it, to see if you can contact a loved one who has passed, or a discarnate mentor. The practice of automatic writing allows you to have your own direct experience of the greater reality. Each of the seven chapters ends with an exercise that builds on the previous ones. At the end of the seventh chapter, you may be ready to take the step outside physical space/time reality and make contact.

The Shift from Upcoming to Current Upheavals

Frances spoke, in *Seven Questions, Book One,* of "upcoming upheavals." The link between "death as transition" and "upcoming upheavals" is not hard to make. In fact, they're not "upcoming" for many people who are already caught up in the effects of climate change, or who are homeless, or who are targets of the hatred and violence that are unleashed when desperate people see no future for themselves.

Are we *all* facing real dangers, real threats to our whole species' existence? How much instability can we withstand? How much temperature increase can we handle? How much suffering can one person experience or witness? Each and every day there are approximately 20 suicides in the US among teenagers, and at least 20 suicides a day of military veterans. That doesn't include the Americans who die from opioid overdoses — 42,000 in 2016.* So much pain is flooding our collective consciousness.

There are many souls who, consciously or intuitively, are trying to steady the ship. But it's rocking precariously and taking on water. We're assuming that the people reading this book still have a place to live, food to eat, some normalcy to cling to. How grateful are we who are fortunate enough to have such continuing stability! Now we are recognizing those who have already lost their homes due to climate chaos, those who are starving, those who are migrating because it's too hot where they are, or because the crops they depend upon cannot grow there anymore. Other places are struggling against the rise of tyranny in their country, opposing it by protesting in the streets — and getting killed. Such unstable situations invite tyrants who take power into their own hands and kill or drive out those who resist. Hence we chose to shift from "upcoming" to "current" in order to remember we are all in this together.

An Evolving Story

We are all participating in, and co-creating, an evolving story of reality. The stories known as the *wisdom traditions* are attempts *at the time of their creation* to describe reality in a coherent narrative. And they share core insights; for example, that Consciousness (or the soul) is primary. Each story of the past drew on the best understanding available at the time, as well as the appropriate symbols and icons of the culture (such as the Bodhi tree, a burning bush, and apparitions of the Virgin Mary). Each story had a good amount of channeled material — that is, new perspective, so as to intrigue the curious. Frances and I are creating the *Seven Questions* series of books to add to a growing literature of the current story. Each story had its limitations — it couldn't be "the whole story," because there *is* no complete story. It will never be complete until there are no more incarnate beings to share it.

The wisdom we need to preserve and hold as part of the story can be safeguarded as we always have — through our great teachers, prophets, and mystics. Now we recognize that there are others such as psychics, mediums, telepaths, remote viewers, and channelers. They can tap the greater realities and report both ancient and contemporary truths we can live by. Scientists in a variety of fields, especially parapsychology, are pushing the boundaries of material reality to reveal a greater reality. They all help put a larger frame on our evolving story.

Book Two Continues the Story

In this book, Frances and I have formulated seven more questions that will help expand your awareness of energies beyond physical matter to Love as our center, and then to the recognition of our own divinity and participation in ongoing creation. The notion of being divine isn't so strange. It simply recognizes that we are co-creators in the *creation of all that is*. Recognizing that is the task at hand. If we can get that one, so much can be improved, remade to fit a more loving, more humane world. There is no hope for fundamental change except for a change in cosmic paradigm — the way we hold our existence.

A spiritual path is both discovery and creation. We discover people who have moved toward Unity Consciousness and we can learn from their reports. Wisdom and Compassion have served all souls who want to move toward the One. Gratitude and Lovingkindness are sources of Light along the way. Our human existence provides a field for our inquiry, where we can learn and practice the qualities of the heart that help us recognize ourselves in each other. Our incarnation on earth also provides us with people, places, and other beings with whom we create community, affording more opportunities to learn from each other.

Outside Sources

In *Book One,* we chose to augment the dialogue between Frances and me with excerpts from other channeled sources. This was meant to show the existence of universal themes that are consistent, even when the sources of the channeled material differ greatly. But all information channeled from the greater reality that has been recorded through the centuries also bears the stamp of the personality of the sender and that of the receiver. Remember that being "on the other side" does not confer omniscience, just a broader frame.

In *Book Two,* there is less channeled material from other sources. Instead, we wanted to emphasize how the messages of this material show up in other forms as well. Here you will find lines of poetry, song lyrics, and contemporary quotes that underscore the existence of a greater reality. We also use stories taken from the daily news to provide an expanded way of understanding space/time events. As we said in *Book One,* this series of books is intended to be an anchor during a chaotic time filled with confusion and suffering. It offers a larger frame, a wider lens, a broader bandwidth, a greater reality.

How to Read This Book: A Quick Review from Book One

Here are some reminders from Book One on how best to use this book on your journey.

- This is a journey of inquiry into the unknown, and so it will contain stretches of uncertainty or doubt for you.

- These insights are not "the truth"; these are ways people have expressed what is true for them.
- A true explorer recognizes and respects the fact that other explorers describe their experiences in terms and images that make sense to them.
- The more we can proceed with an open heart and open mind into the next phase of our collective spiritual journey — to evolve with the divine within us — the more joyful, the more magnificent our homecoming will be when we make the transition to the greater reality that awaits us all.

Seven New Questions

Each of the seven questions in *Book One* became an entry point for trying to grasp dimensions beyond our limited ability to comprehend. For *Book Two*, we stay the course by taking each question into a deeper place of exploration. So the first question in *Book One* — *Am I more than my physical body?* — becomes *What Is Aliveness?* in *Book Two*. Again, as each of the seven questions is introduced, you'll find one explorer's answer to that question, in the form of a quotation. We encourage you to find your own way to answer it.

Here are the seven questions from *Book One*:

1. **Am I more than my physical body?**
2. **What's it like "on the other side"?**
3. **What presence fills the universe? God? Oneness? Love?**
4. **How can I *know* there is a greater reality?**
5. **Why does someone incarnate?**

6. **How does one live with the knowledge that there is life after life?**

7. **Where is Home?**

And here are the seven questions addressed in *Book Two*:

1. **What is Aliveness?**
2. **How do we let go of the fear of death?**
3. **How do we participate as co-creators of reality?**
4. **How can we contact the other side?** *The practice of automatic writing*
5. **What are we here to learn?**
6. **How do we live our purpose during the upheavals?**
7. **What is time-bound? What is eternal?**

Text Notes: "C:" indicates that Cynthia is the speaker. "F:" indicates Frances is the speaker. Words in brackets [ ] were added by C for greater clarity; F's words are verbatim except for very minor editing; [smile] came through from Frances as a feeling tone. In several instances, Frances gave me a direct experience of what she was describing. It was wordless — just a glimpse of knowing — beyond any words I have to express it.

Words or phrases marked by * indicate that a further explanation can be found in the **Glossary** or **Endnotes**.

What is aliveness?

≈

You are creatures of light. From light have you come, to light shall you go, and surrounding you through every step is the light of your infinite being.... Know that ever about you stands the reality of love, and each moment you have the power to transform your world by what you have learned.

— RICHARD BACH, *One*

In *Seven Questions: Book One*, the opening question was: Am I more than my physical body? The answer was a resounding Yes! that echoed throughout the book. In returning to Question 1 and expanding on it, we come to Aliveness. This abstract word describes a sense of being that transcends the categories of incarnate/discarnate.

As Frances puts it: "What is Aliveness but a knowing that we are immortal beings, always welcome into the Beloved Community? It also comes from Compassion — the experience of another's pain. Aliveness emanates from the heart, and expands its territory, so to speak, with every service deed, with every kind word, or even a silent gift of recognition of each other's divinity."

⁓⊚

*(**F** = Frances; **C** = Cynthia)*

C: Most people who knew you as Frances Vaughan while you were here on earth now believe that you are dead. I, and others you've contacted, know that you're alive. What does that mean to you?

F: Being alive in this dimension proximate to Earth — actually interwoven — is a joy and a burden. It's a joy to be free of the burdens of physical existence — the sorrows and losses, the aches and pains of aging.

But it's a different kind of burden to be so close and yet so far. I'm choosing, as many other souls have also, to stay close to loved ones still incarnate. To help guide as much as we are allowed and can do, and to still influence the world of physical matter and unexpected tragedies. From our perspective, it has so much to recommend it — the ebb and flow of human values, the richness of the lives people lead when they're fully engaged with the challenges of earth incarnation.

We are every bit as alive as you are, only more so because we know that physical death is a setup in the space/time world. It both challenges beings to see what they can accomplish while alive [on earth]. It also reins most people in to a limited amount of things they can count on. A built-in limitation to push against.

What a glorious feeling it is to climb a mountain, have a baby, finish a painting, knowing that death could happen to prevent it, and taking that chance, that opportunity to be more Alive. So too, we in this dimension know our limits, push against them. Not because we're risking death. We know it doesn't exist. But the difference here is the "push" to become more aware of the divinity of the whole ongoing enterprise (for lack of a better word).

We want more and more of the Love, the Light, and yes, the taste of divinity — our own consciousness of being co-creators of the Whole. It's like any artist or musician or engineer who wants their contribution to be as superb and elegant as it can be. We're busy *perfecting* (again for lack of a better word) ourselves as an art form as well as the collaboration that is our soul group. It's glorious fun, and challenging.

Earth provides a kind of workout that measures contributions. Here there are no measuring sticks. There's an internal knowing that we are moving in consciousness toward merging with the All That Is. We have all the time and space [we need], which doesn't exist here except as creations. We can put on a play that has a beginning and an ending. But anyone who cares to, can see the ending first. It's all happening at once. Hard to describe until you get here.

So Aliveness is this participation in collective creation. Choose your medium. Try something new. Nothing stops you, as [it does] on earth.

C: That sounds dizzying, like too much going on at once.

F: It would seem so to an incarnate visitor. That's why, when someone who has a near-death experience (NDE)* comes to visit, we slow it down to their level of perception. Otherwise, it would be a blur. And if they are going back to their incarnation, we want to give them a glimpse of what's to come for them, so they can report back.

Many Dimensions of Existence

C: Can you say more about what it means to "be alive?"

F: Extravaganza! A multitude of persons who all participate as [members of] one inviolate soul. We are such a conglomeration, a symphony, a mélange. No earth words can capture it. The knowledge of ourselves [on earth] as one incarnate person is beautiful. I don't in any way mean to diminish it. Each and every being is a gem, human and otherwise. But when you cross over to this dimension — and this is very modest compared to what lies ahead for each of us — you experience an expanded awareness that only begins to show you (and me) the promise of aliveness, so unsurpassed by any stretch of the imagination.

C: Wow! You're right. As you communicate to me, I get a much larger and grander sense of reality. The words can hardly begin to describe it. It comes without words. Just impressions and feelings. What else can you say about being alive?

F: The dexterity we have to have to create any setting, any event — an orchestration of flowers, for instance. I always appreciate the "creative ones" on earth — the painters, sculptors, musicians, and so on. [But] we are *all* creators here. First of all, we co-create beautiful facades of places we remember, or fantastical ones. In our own ways, we add imaginative pieces to the Whole. The amazing thing is that it all fits together like a puzzle, no piece out of place. It's the Communion of the all-pervasive Oneness, God, that makes it all so harmonious.

C: Do all souls participate in this glorious creation?

F: No, I'm afraid not. I'm fortunate to have existed through enough lifetimes — schools of learning — to have been able to come into this dimension rather easily. That does not in any way negate the souls who are in more difficult dimensions who are receiving [what might be called] "rehab."* There are souls in so many different stages of development, certainly way beyond where I am now. But I can taste, I can sense those higher dimensions and understand there is a process of unfoldment in all of this. There is a *telos*, a drive to become a fully divine participant in the All That Is. It includes an understanding, and many experiences, of different situations — on earth and elsewhere.

C: It sounds as though you and I are able to communicate because you are where you are. Not struggling, but not so advanced that you've left earth and its incarnations behind.

F: Yes, that's right. You and I are in perfect balance to be able to do this work. I'm close enough, right in a parallel universe to yours. And you have reached out to get beyond the space/

time construct and made contact. This would not be happening if you did not believe it could happen.

You think because you've read some Jane Roberts/Seth* books plus others on channeling that this portal became available to you. Not so. You've been grooming yourself for this purpose for many lifetimes. When you're on this side you'll see them all.

C: What do you make of a lifetime on earth? It's so "real" and has so many wonderful and terrible aspects. Putting a larger frame on it all, to include your dimension and beyond, seems like an excursion, a vacation. Maybe we incarnates should just focus on *this* dimension while we're here.

F: That's what the great majority of people do. And God blesses them for it. If everyone was flying around out-of-body, or contacting spirits, or trying on other dimensions, the whole enterprise would collapse. Someone has to "keep the lights on" and do all the necessary functions to keep the planet intact as possible.

That, in fact, is what's happening. It's a consensus reality with the participants *creating* the reality, or realities, if you recognize that all incarnates do not share the same one. There are many versions of space/time. However, when things start to fall apart, as they now are in your dimension, interventions are made. And they're made with people like yourself who are willing to be a bridge to a greater reality. A messenger, so to speak.

Rebalance is Happening Now

F: The situations that will arise soon in your reality will tax so many souls. The idea of "why bother" will come to many. "It's all falling apart." Why make the effort to stay alive? Why try to be of service to others who are in pain, or suffering from the Four Horsemen* riding over the world?

Your life will become more meaningful if you can see what's going on in the larger frame of necessary destruction that makes room for new creations. Humans have pushed way past the "carrying capacity" of earth in terms of spaces to live and resources to support that population. A reset has to happen. When certain individuals can put a larger frame on what's going on, it will provide comfort and more importantly, courage and fortitude to carry on as long as possible. The goal is a more harmonious and loving place to be. Much adjustment has to happen to reach that new equilibrium.

C: And my guess is that it involves much suffering and death also.

F: Historical resets have always had those aspects. Experiencing death is something that every soul on earth today has done many times. Some in horrible ways. Yet most choose to return, to finish their education of the whole of existence. Nothing is ever destroyed, not humans, not other species, not other energy forms that you don't know about yet. It all goes through what you might call a transformation process.

C: What does that mean?

F: Every single molecule and cell and microorganism, to use tiny examples, are parts of a living system that is not static. They are all involved in an ever-changing, reconfiguring, alive organism. You are a part of that, and now you know that you won't die, just a change of address, while the "stuff" that formed your body and physical world goes on to new forms.

Having that knowledge when things get rough, as they will for most everyone, will be so useful. It will give the ones who experience those travails a strong sense of going home, of staying bonded to loved ones [still incarnate] and others who are waiting "on the other side," as we described in *Book One*. So much easier to take the events in stride when you can hold that perspective.

"Sustaining the Gaze," as the Buddhists Say

C: It's so hard to focus on all the suffering that's going on.

F: All necessary, I'm afraid.

C: Why?

F: Because the machinations of the human forces have caused great distress to the soul of the planet. It's struggling to take the continuous assaults — the disregard of humans for its welfare. It must stop. It will stop. It will be stopped.

C: But why do seemingly innocent creatures have to suffer so much for human greed and mindlessness? It seems so unfair.

F: You're forgetting that it is all of a piece. There is no separation between humans and the other creatures. They reflect human attributes and creativity. But it is all One. So those "external" or objective pieces of the human consciousness are trying to tell the humans something: "Pay attention. Look what you're doing to this beautiful creation. You're destroying it, at least for the time being, until it can regenerate itself." That may take millions of years.

C: Sometimes it feels hopeless to try to fix anything.

F: Quite the contrary. Many souls can evolve more rapidly during a period like this because they are stretched to expand heart and mind and consciousness way beyond normal levels to accommodate the enormity of what's going on.

C: And yet you said [in *Book One*] the best approach is to be in the present moment. Take what's happening on a moment-to-moment level.

F: Yes. The challenge is always to balance the space/time dimension — and all that's going on — within the larger frame that sees it all as a learning experience, as a moral gymnasium [as mentioned in *Book One*]. Because we are souls first, citizens of a nonphysical reality, and bodies (some of us) only secondarily, we can have some comfort in knowing this particularly painful period of Earth's history will end, as it always does, with a redressing of the imbalance and a return to a stasis of life — all aspects of life in harmony with each other.

That will happen. It's built into the design. But not in a time frame that someone looking from a single lifetime can fathom. If a majority of people could see the suffering and cruel deaths as parts of themselves — interior, not exterior — it could be stopped quickly. I'm afraid, correct that, I *know* that's not going to happen.

Physical Body as Expression of Soul

C: If we are going to shake people's world, or more correctly, say that upheavals will be doing that soon, if not already, we need to give them some ground to stand on. What do you think?

F: Absolutely. Each individual needs to contact the essential being that they each are. That is the being that is Alive, who will experience "life after life" and know themselves as particles of God.

You have to find that inner being, the larger soul group that exists outside of space/time. You have to get past the limitation of seeing yourself as physical first, and spirit or soul second. Unless you find *I am the I AM,* you will have a terrible time when the upheavals touch you directly, as so many already know.

C: Can we say more about *I am the I AM*? My psychic counselor suggested it to me as a mantra. She said I should repeat it and look into a mirror while doing so. I haven't done it much. I found it difficult to do. What is it and how do we arrive at that knowing?

F: It is the gift of God touching you and communicating to you: You and I are One. Not separate, not a fragment, not a reflection. You are divine. So am I. The *I am* is the recognition, the experience, the deep knowing of your eternal soul. It is a coming out from behind a physical human [who's] caught in the matrix of space/time, realizing that I am much more than that shard, beautiful as it might be.

It's the answer to *Book One,* Question 1: Am I more than my physical body? The answer is a resounding Yes. Once you can say that with no equivocation, no disclaimers, no doubts, you have transcended the temporary boundary between the physical and all other forms of being available to us. We are SO much more than physical. It's like your little finger thinking it's the whole you. It's an important part, but so much a fraction of who you are.

I am the I AM means you feel you live your larger self while at the same time playing the role you've chosen during your incarnation.

The first exercise that we will offer on how to begin a practice of automatic writing is, in fact, the process of getting in touch with your larger being. If you didn't go beyond Step 1 [exercise at end of this chapter], but mastered it, you will have benefited greatly from reading this book.

Just that reversal of sensibility — not "I am a physical being expanding myself into a nonphysical reality." NO. I am a nonphysical being, expressing myself into the space/time dimension. Just get that and you [the reader] will have accomplished the basic task of moving toward the greater reality.

C: Most of us have been taught from childhood that we are separate from what constitutes the divine. I do understand that the mantra is the affirmation, the acknowledgment that I am not limited to a physical body. But I can't comfortably repeat that mantra yet.

F: If you can't comfortably say *I am the I AM*, that is, go to that level of revelation, then it will happen in some other dimension, or lifetime. "*I am the I AM*." Keep practicing that one to make it the musical mantra of your soul. It's always been true. You're just calling it into consciousness within your being.

C: It has an ego-inflating aspect to it, doesn't it?

F: No, not if you hold it as a reality that you have nothing to do with creating. You are a creator of the cosmos (to use a term). You can participate in its evolution, in its explosion into a much more wise and expansive being. But I'm afraid you can't take credit for [its] coming into being. You didn't create your own soul. God did. *I am the I Am* means you recognize your divinity, your timelessness, your membership in your oversoul,* and its membership in the All-in-One.

Earth Has Ground Rules

C: What else can we say about being co-creators while we exist in space/time on earth?

F: Imagine a beautiful parkland, a place where many other species co-habit their environment.

C: Are they co-creating it?

F: Of course. All the interaction, including predator/prey, are neatly folded into an environment where the ground rules are understood, and within which each creature has a measure of freedom, and a measure of habit, instinct, and genetic understanding of how to be here now. Humans have a greater measure of freedom. We call it "free will." When given an environment where the rules are looser, we can create more beauty — or more mischief.

C: Are we humans the superior species on planet earth?

F: I think we will find out we are not. But it depends on what the criteria for "superior" means. Best at building habitats, places to live? No, I don't think so. Bees and termites create architectural wonders. Best at living in harmony with the Earth's other species, and land forms, and processes like weather and volcanoes? I think not.

We are what we are... a unique species trying to see if we can continue to exist on this planet. Maybe. Maybe not. There are easier planets to live on. [Remember that] separate planets are an illusion. As souls looking to evolve ourselves toward the Oneness of Being, toward recognizing our connection to the Divine, we can choose different forms of incarnation — try on different dimensions, if you will. It's not like someone could choose Mars, or some exoplanet that astronomers have discovered is "Earth-like." That is misleading. Just as you experience living on earth as a real experience, you can have other "real" experiences in a dimension that has space/time parameters. But you're not literally living on some other planet in the universe. Is that clear?

C: Yes, thank you very much. How are you doing in the dimension you're in now?

F: I'm in heaven. All the descriptions from ancient writings, and reports from visitations, as in NDEs, don't begin to capture the exquisite dimensions of where I reside for the present moment. We progress at our own pace into more and more wondrous ways to exist and to experience our Aliveness. Nothing prepared me for this, except that as my larger soul group, I have been here before. But Frances Vaughan is enjoying it as if it's her first time. In some ways it is because it too is evolving, being co-created by all of us here. It bubbles with creativity.

Speaking of the *I am the I AM*, as we were, it's so apparent that I am a part of a larger One, an All That Is that is everything and no-thing. At some point all the fabrications fall away and all that's left is an incomprehensible Oneness, a Nothingness that holds the potential for everything. But there is no material sensibility here, just Love and Joy and Being. That is what awaits most everyone who will experience, or who are experiencing the current upheavals on earth. If you can grow into a sense of how temporary it [a lifetime] is, your trip across the bridge will be so much easier.

Here is the first exercise of *Seven Questions, Book Two.* In this book, there will be one exercise, how to begin *automatic writing*, divided into the seven chapters. We strongly suggest that you take the time to master each step before you attempt your first automatic writing experience. Just as you would start with the basics in learning any new activity — for instance, taking the time to learn the musical scales before you try a whole melody.

All seven steps can be found listed together in the back material.

....

OPENING EXERCISE: (STEP 1)

Sit in a quiet, comfortable place where you won't be disturbed. If you have a practice of meditation, begin that process of clearing your mind. If you're not accustomed to doing this, it will take a few minutes longer. Let go of all other concerns and thoughts. Watch yourself breathe in and out slowly, with your abdomen rising and falling. Make sure your body is completely relaxed. Check for tension first in your lower body, then in your upper body. Then imagine that you occupy more space than simply your physical body. Your consciousness extends beyond your body.

If you feel yourself getting nervous, stop at this point.

Repeat the opening part of the exercise (clearing your mind, watching your breath, imagining your consciousness extending beyond your body) until you are centered and ready to **name** the contact you would like to make. This could be your higher self, a spirit guide, or someone who was incarnate and has passed on. Keep holding that open field, and let your choice of contact show up. Do not try to "think it." Let it appear. Hold the intention of contacting your desired connection. Ask yourself why you are seeking this experience. Repeat this exercise in upcoming days until you feel completely comfortable with your sense of an expanded self, and your choice of contact.

If it happens that you start receiving a telepathic message that seems to be coming from another source, then you are on your way. Go to *Seven Steps to Automatic Writing* on p. 159 to find suggestions for opening the conversation. Most people who begin this process do not receive an immediate response. But don't rule it out.

....

How do we let go of the fear of death?

~

"The reason why death is no longer frightening as all of these [near-death] excerpts express, is that after his experience a person no longer entertains any doubts about his survival of bodily death. It is no longer merely an abstract possibility to him, but a fact of his experience."

— DR. RAYMOND MOODY, *Life After Life*

Can you imagine living your life without the fear of death? Can you imagine living with the strong sense that you are carrying on the work of this lifetime, and when it's over, your existence in this space/time reality is ended? Can you ever be OK with that? This does not mean that you don't care about how much suffering your death may entail.

This does not mean that you will not feel deep pain from the letting go of loved ones. Those considerations have to do with *dying*. The question "How do we let go of the fear of death?" has to do with *death* — that time, that life, as you know it, ends.

People who have reported a near-death experience or had strong communications from someone "on the other side" have often commented afterwards that their fear of death is greatly diminished. Dr. Kenneth Ring, a leading NDE researcher, has spent over 40 years interviewing NDE survivors and has written several books on the subject. In his book, *waiting to die*, he commented on how that changed his perception of an afterlife:

> [W]hen I go to my death, I will go convinced that my end will not result in my personal extinction but in my absorption into the world radiant Light and all-encompassing unconditional love that so many near-death experiencers have encountered when they pass temporarily into the realm beyond this life.

C: Frances, how does someone let go of the fear of death?

F: Imagine a building, one you know well, in your neighborhood. Get a good image of it. Now imagine it gone. Simply missing. A hole where it used to be. It's unnerving. It raises issues of identity and security. Here yesterday, gone today. That's why Buddhists spend time contemplating impermanence. Any physical object, or person, or system could end tomorrow. Could you imagine dying tomorrow? You might say: "But I have so much to take care of. Who will do it?" Or, "I have to finish this work — only I can. I can't think about not being here."

Some people arrange to have a slow death to adjust themselves, and those around them, to their soon-to-be absence. Some leave in a flash — a terrible accident, massive heart attack, getting murdered while walking down a dangerous street. So many ways to die quickly. Hard on those around them, as we see those stories every day. But far easier on the individual who doesn't like long goodbyes.

C: Do we really get to orchestrate the timing? Long and fading, or gone in an instant?

F: Of course. We have total control over when and where we die. Not in specific details, like which car runs over you in a crosswalk. But knowing that you will die soon in an "accident."

C: My cousin recently died in what seemed like a very short time, a few hours after having what was diagnosed as a massive heart attack. She was talking to her sister by video connection early one evening. Then several hours later she was dead. Did she know she was going to die that night?

F: Knowing is a tricky word. On what level did she know? As in "It's time for breakfast" or "It is time to die"? No, not that level of awareness. Our greater consciousness, the one we share with all other beings, incarnate and discarnate loved ones, has a "knowing" that isn't bound by time or space. That level is aware of everything that's impacting you and what you're impacting around you as well.

C: Can we know if our death is near?

F: Yes. *I* did. But you have to be able to break down the barriers that prevent you from seeing or knowing it. Some people get premonitions of their impending death, and it comes true. Again you have to be open to the information. Very few are. Actually it's not necessary, because it will happen as anticipated by your higher Self. Having advance knowledge of its timing might prompt you to "have your papers in order." People who have responsibilities to others — spouses, family members and so on — often do a better job of leaving helpful directives available. But single people, living alone, are prone to put it off, and off, and off. One day it's too late, as your younger cousin found out when her older sister died.

The world is a messy place. If we were all very orderly about papers in order and funeral arrangements made in advance, how dull it would all be.

All you need to do, what's most important about preparations for death, is the understanding that death of the body is natural, certainly inevitable. The soul goes on to a nearby dimension for reunion with its soul group, and reflections and rest. You can count on it. Getting to that level of acceptance is what we're trying to help with by putting together these thoughts into a book.

We are not talking about some passive death here — "I think I'll die today because it's easier than living in this lifetime." NO. There's a promise of life to come, but the purpose of your life and the moral character you develop while incarnate are crucial to how well you will arrive on the other side. By that I mean that everyone is welcomed back with loving arms extended. But having discovered a deeper meaning of being in unity with other parts of your soul who are waiting and directly sharing in the benefit of your lifetime — that is immeasurable.

Again, everyone is welcomed back. But to bring a deeper sense of the love of God, love of others, love of the Whole without exception, is a blessing that extends to all members of your soul group and then ripples out to your oversoul — the grouping of other souls you belong to.

C: I know the terms we are using — soul group and oversoul — are abstract but the best we can do right now. Are you aware of more accurate, or more descriptive terms that could help us understand more deeply?

F: No. Because there are no words formed yet in the language we are using that would make sense to anyone. I could make up a word — *greckle* — to say that's how souls relate, but it doesn't help at all. Do you see what I mean?

C: Yes. It must be terribly frustrating to know more from where you are and not have a better way of describing it, given the pool of words at our disposal.

F: That's why we must continue to insist on experience — direct experience — as a way to get past the paucity of words.

Right After Death of the Body

F: Also we need to finish the story, the story of what happens in the immediate period after the soul is free from the body. As I've said, it's not as easy as it might sound. Some NDE people make it sound like a walk in the park, only better. Actually, it's quite scary and disorienting even for those well prepared. The ego and the survival mechanisms in place don't acquiesce gracefully.

A psychic development well worth cultivating is a face-to-face encounter with death on its terms. You can do that by volunteering for hospice, although you're not present for many deaths. The more challenging activity is contemplating your own death: *I won't be here anymore. I will be dead. The world and my loved ones will carry on without me.*

How does that feel? Someone with low self-worth will say that's fine. But if you value your contribution and feel you have more to give, more love to share, more being to experience, it will be sad, at best, to contemplate. But intolerable to those who don't have a strong sense of life after life.

What Happens "On the Other Side?"

C: What can we expect when we enter "the other side?"

F: Confusion. [Asking] "Where am I?" Even the souls who have done it a million times still come out of the darkened tunnel into the bright sunlight, to use an analogy, and can't see much.

There are welcomers. Loved ones who had passed before. Spirit guides who have been with you since your birth. But it's so different, so dazzling in some ways that you're bewildered and maybe even frightened.

C: What's there to be frightened of?

F: Loss of control — as much as you thought you had while you were incarnate. The more you have prepared yourself before dying to know you are re-entering a greater reality, the more calm you'll be. If you've been telling yourself all your adult life that there's nothing after death, then you will be bewildered at such a grand and glorious plane of existence. Of course you'll be led in gradually. But after a long passageway or tunnel to get through, you begin to "see the light at the end of the tunnel." [smile] That's one of the most accurate and descriptive phrases [in any language].

Then gradually, the scene in front of you starts to come into focus. And there it is — not the static image of old paintings — [instead] a place vibrant with colors you've never seen, sounds you've never heard.

You still have your own mind, your own thoughts. Those aren't taken away. But the mind could be "blown," as they say, if you've been holding a rather narrow or small view of the afterlife. Or held none at all.

C: What about souls who "have some hell to pay," as was mentioned in *Book One*?

F: We don't have to go into that because they won't be reading this book.

C: That sounds like an easy out for us. Can we say any more?

F: The Life Review section of *Book One** gives some details. In a short summary, let's say every soul goes through a life review when the soul has acclimated to the new surroundings. All the actions, thoughts, behaviors you've ever had or done flash by. You experience the pain you've caused and the joys you've created for yourself and others. It's like a final examination for that lifetime. But there is no pass or fail. We all pass on to our soul group, then group soul, and what each soul has deemed their "home." There is a sense of Justice here, but it's God's Justice. The kind that looks squarely at the behavior and offers forgiveness and mercy in exchange for remorse and contrition, and a remedying of the situation, like community service but much more specific to actual behavior.

People share stories of wonderful experiences on earth. They also tell of terrible things they did and had to make amends for after they died.

C: What kind of "amends"?

F: Actually taking the place of the person who was hurt and re-living the experiences of the one on the receiving end. That's one kind of amends.

Another is recognizing a person who suffered, not directly from anything I did or didn't do as an omission, but whose life was impacted by my thoughtlessness or being oblivious to their situation. It's learning compassion from the standpoint of feeling the pain truly, feeling it as suffering.

You want to say, "I'm so sorry. I wish I had known that a kindness from me, a recognition of your divinity, your invio-late soul, would have helped you so much. Instead, I ignored you. Walked right by. Even thought unkind thoughts about how you should get a job." [smile]

We underestimate how much we can do by giving our attention, our recognition of another's dignity as a being. Instead, we often diminish the other by seeing the unat-tractive covering and judging [him or her] by their cover, and not by their roles in the co-creation.

C: Thank you for the review of that. It's good to keep it in memory as part of our story, as we cross over and leave our incarnation.

F: Yes, and it's only a gloss of a description. It's so much more intense and detailed than we can possibly describe. Each life review is unique because each soul is unique.

How to Live Before You Die

C: What other principles do we need to tell our readers of *Book Two*?

F: One principle will be to stay the course. Whatever you are doing to keep the integrity of the Whole, keep doing it as long as you can. Parenting, teaching, repairing phone lines, working at a carwash — all are contributions, every one of them important. Not only for their function, but for their [evolutionary] *value* — the quality of perseverance, doing your activity with Love, Integrity, and Wholesomeness.

C: What's Wholesomeness? That's a new word.

F: It's my way of saying "working for the whole." You know how wisdom is often defined as understanding what's good for the collective, not necessarily what's best for the individual? Remember the biblical story of King Solomon — two mothers are claiming a child and Solomon said, "Let's cut him in half." "Oh no," said the real mother. "I'd rather let him go with her than kill him." Solomon declared the woman who showed compassion to be the true mother, and gave her the whole child.*

Wisdom will be sorely needed in the upcoming chaos. People [will be needed] who see what needs to be done to save the species, as opposed to saving individuals. Just as leaders have had to make decisions to send young people into war, knowing that some or many will die. What a terrible decision to have to make! But one that's necessary to preserve a country or a culture. Then there are those leaders who send their people to their deaths in order to plunder, to conquer territory, to take power over.

Wisdom is necessary to sort out those motives to see what's what. Not always clear and clean. Gandhi was clear. So was Hitler in his intent. Where would wisdom choose to be? Not always so clear cut [as in those two examples]. The US had mixed motives in its recent wars.

C: Can we ask for help in determining the wise decision?

F: Of course. And those of us on this side are as ready as we can be. But we can only help if asked. We cannot intervene unilaterally without the participation on your side. Then we can act in concert with you.

C: What else should we focus on?

F: The twin companion of Wisdom is Compassion. Where they are in balance, you can expect the best possible outcome. Maybe not what you'd hoped for, but balanced and life-affirming — the best path forward. Developing Compassion for others' suffering. For yourself and for all your loved ones in their various reactions to very different situations. Maybe someone you know, even someone you love, is going to go in a direction of personal survival, or violence that you cannot abide. Having compassion for the person who makes choices hurtful to others is absolutely necessary. It will tax you and many you know. It's all part of the lessons to be learned at this juncture in your evolution, which of course includes the evolution of all species and the Earth itself.

C: It feels like it will be such a sad and scary time.

F: It will be. That's precisely why the message of these books, and many others in process right now, are so necessary. Many people will be comforted, and find a deeper level of courage in knowing that death is a transition to a greater reality — one where all the sadness and frightening aspects of a current incarnation dissipate. And [that] you are welcomed back home.

Ride the Waves

C: What else would you like to share tonight?

F: We're in a vortex of energy right now. Here too since I've chosen to stay close to the earth plane. It's heating up and promises to explode into good and bad pieces that will go their own ways. Which "probable reality" one ends up in will be determined by the mindset of each being involved. Many will want a kinder, gentler way of being. Some will want the aggressive predator/prey model, and they will find it. Some will not know what to do and will latch onto whatever promises security. They will be the ones who have not remembered that an incarnation is temporary. One of many incarnations, whether in linear time or simultaneously, depending on vantage point.

C: You mentioned that there were forces "on your side" working to extend the knowledge of the greater reality so it's more broadly known and accepted.

F: We're working on it.

C: Who's "we?"

F: Those forces who want this message of hope and greater perspective to provide comfort to those who must go through a period of suffering, loss, fright, grief. The forces are in motion. How many people will rise to the occasion of "first responder," or caretaker, or peacemaker? We don't know.

We must stop the divisiveness, the hatred, the right-and-wrong judgments. Only a message of Love will truly work. Forget the rest. It's not as important as the preservation of what is best in the human species. That's worth saving, and it's the only thing worth working toward.

C: How does one balance knowledge of the current upheavals and crumbling infrastructure with a sense of centeredness and equanimity?

F: What I have to say tonight may not answer your question, but it will address it.

If you're in a small boat and it's rocking from side to side with rough waves, you find a way to set your body and move with the motion of the waves. A master sailor does not control the wind and waves. A master sailor knows how to ride and become one with those forces. So too with many amusement rides that ask you to ride with the forces — downhill, around curves. But you know you're safe because of the design of the ride. The design of a lifetime is to be buffeted by various forces, be rocked by the waves and the losses. But knowing the design, that you're an immortal being and even if you lose your body — or when you do — you experience some disorientation and then you move to another form of existence.

I don't know how to say it more clearly, but knowing that death is a transition to life after life, to returning to your soul group, to being Home with your group soul... all that should be as comforting as you can achieve within your current lifetime. If you are reading this book, trying the exercises, then you are at least curious. [Ask yourself:] "Is this a cosmology — that is, a way of explaining existence that has truth in it?"

It isn't more complicated than that at this point in human evolution. It's just very difficult to hold onto with the assault of materialism — [the belief that] physical space/time is all there is.

It's difficult because anything that smacks of religion is suspect these days, given how some traditions have fallen into disrepair. Each one has a shard of truth, a sense of practices that can hold you through turbulence. But they don't hold up well in the face of assaults of consumerism, massive entertainment complexes meant to dull the mind and spirit. Those are powerful. And some people are seduced by science and don't see its limits, or have adopted it as their religion.

C: Holding the strong belief of life after life needs to be able to stand up to watching immense suffering, loss of loved ones before your eyes. The loss of everything you count on in the face of fires and floods and violence of all kinds.

F: That's why belief isn't what we're suggesting. We're suggesting *experiences* of the greater reality, and a very deep knowing that you will reunite with loved ones on the other side. That deep knowing comes from experience, and we will provide more suggestions for portals tailored to that kind of deep knowledge.

C: We provided a variety of portals, some tippy-toe, some more advanced, in *Book One*. Can you suggest one that provides a good access to the knowledge we're talking about now?

F: Yes. It has to do with allowing yourself to go beyond your safe zone, your comfort zone, your strongly held beliefs.

C: How does one do that?

F: Go to Nothingness. Find a quiet place to sit and begin with a meditative clearing. Then say to yourself: "I wish to let go of all beliefs I have, just for this practice time, of how the world exists, what is reality, what happens when you die." It may take several different attempts just to get to that space.

Then allow in one thought: *I am Divine. I am the I AM.* Let that one thought fill the space — the whole space — that had been occupied with those earlier thoughts. That again may take several sessions.

Then ask for help from God, from your spirit guides, from whatever trustworthy source you know: "Show me how I exist beyond space and time. Let me leave this reality and all its seductions and get a brief glimpse of the greater reality."

It will happen. It will take concerted effort. And you will receive the gift of nothingness.

C: That sounds like it might be akin to deep meditation within the wisdom traditions. Is it the same?

F: It may be for some people. But you don't have to spend months in retreat or years of practice to get there. Access to the greater reality is experienced by millions of people who don't have those traditional practices. They simply set themselves up, as in an outdoor setting, or inside a cathedral or mosque or temple, and hold the intention of having that experience. The greater reality is proximate; it's nearby. Then you have a new foundation, a deeper one than the old collection of beliefs, upon which to build a new understanding. No religion, no dogma, just a direct experience of how you are not your body, or even your mind. You are an immortal part of all that is. When you have that to rely on because you've truly incorporated it into your being, then you will ride the waves. The waves won't go away. Loss, grief, suffering, horror, as we see so much of breaking out all over the world. Those events will still be there. But now you're riding in the larger vehicle, the one that will get you safely through this lifetime and into the next.

C: That was very helpful and provided a good basis for answering my question of accessing a greater reality. Thank you!

....

EXERCISE: (STEP 2)

Raising your vibrational level: Your intention is to make contact at the highest possible level of your soul's development. You are focused entirely on an inner space. Locate that spark of divinity that resides in each and every soul. Let that spark expand until it turns into a strong sense of Light emanating from you. Fill yourself with the presence of Love that permeates the universe. Deeply sense that this exercise in making connection with nonphysical spirits has happened easily for millions of people throughout time. It is about opening, not efforting.

Focus on your intention to contact someone through automatic writing. You will succeed if you ask respectfully and your intention is to benefit your highest self and also be in service to All That Is.

Repeat Steps 1 and 2 in the upcoming days until you feel completely at ease and ready to go on.

....

—Question 3—

How do we participate as co-creators of reality?

∿

"When you enter time and physical life, you are already aware of its conditions. You are biologically and psychologically predisposed to grow within that rich environment, to contribute on all levels to the fulfillment of your species — but more than this, to add your own unique viewpoint and experience to the greater patterns of consciousness of which you are part....

"When you fulfill your own abilities, when you express your personal idealism through acting it out to the best of your ability in your daily life, then you are changing the world for the better."

— JANE ROBERTS/SETH, *The Individual and the Nature of Mass Events*

S ome of our readers might remember a saying popular in the 1980s "You create your own reality." To some, it was "truth." To others, it was the height of the silly New Age. How does it look from here?

Frances has already said that in the dimension she's in, there is an overall sense of co-creation. She'll elaborate on that here. What about creating our own physical space/time reality? In a word, it's *complicated*. Many philosophy books and whole religions are devoted to what's real and what's illusion. The theme of *Book Two* is: Consciousness creates physical forms. Rather than having an abstract discussion, Frances and I will take a look at how our thoughts function to define the world around us, and what *co-creation* means in practical terms.

꘠

C: Do our thoughts create reality for ourselves?

F: Thoughts create each person's reality. I am creating my reality in this dimension and have chosen to stay in an earth-like dimension during our work together. Here we can design any form we want. I've chosen a comfortable dwelling and lots of flowers in and outside, as well as gardens, much like the Tiburon house.*

C: You are making it sound like we can create our own reality while incarnate. If I want to have a hot fudge sundae, can I make it happen "out of thin air?"

F: If someone presents you with a golden flute, could you play a beautiful melody?

C: I don't think so.

F: If someone asked you to write a treatise on how the planet Earth evolves in cycles, could you do it?

C: I don't think so.

F: Exactly. You don't think so. As much as you might wish for an ice cream sundae to show up, you don't think you could do it, right?

C: Right. But people see themselves during dreams doing things like playing piano that they can't do in space/time.

F: And some of them move into that ability. In space/time you have to practice. That means not only mastering the technique. It means, more importantly, shifting to a belief — a set of thoughts that form belief — and it becomes their reality. Don't underestimate the creation of the belief — "I can do this." It's a slow process, not instantaneous as you're suggesting, but it has the core characteristic of "I can make it happen."

I wouldn't have expected to create my own reality — my living quarters — if I hadn't been shown by so many others in this dimension how it works, and again most importantly, that it can be done. We're advised to think about it first and do some planning so it comes out to our liking. [smile]

C: I see. So I probably shouldn't waste my time manufacturing a sundae out of thin air. I might try something that has some social value.

F: Jesus twice fed multitudes with a few loaves of bread and fishes.

C: That was a miracle.

F: That's what people called it when they have no understanding of how we can co-create reality with our thoughts. Incarnates do it all the time.

C: Is "thinking" really the operative term? Is it our thoughts that create any reality around us, whatever dimension we're in?

F: That's as close as we can get to describing a mechanism. No, it's not simply thoughts like "I want to manifest a red rose." There are a host of factors that come together to create a textured reality, not the least of which is our soul group's level of evolution. The concept of "thoughts" is as close as it gets in terms of describing the creation of other realities. But there are dynamics for which your Earth languages have no names or even awareness of. So here we are again. Trying to use three-dimensional words to describe something much more expansive.

What Is Consensus Reality?

C: Please explain "consensus reality" — the level of consciousness we have in day-to-day activities. We all seem to be sharing an agreed-upon version of reality — "The chair is there. It's raining outside," and so on.

F: Yes. That's what it takes to create an environment where you test yourself against what you and others have created. You could create your own reality — just for yourself. But then everything would work the way *you* wanted it to. You incarnate on earth to learn how to navigate your own journey through *other people's* constructions as well as your own. Can you maintain your focus, your values, your purpose in life, your relationships, your health in an environment filled with other people's versions of reality? That's the challenge, or fun, or failure of living a life.

By the way, don't forget Thomas Edison. Failure can teach us as much as success. What a contribution! How many light bulbs did Edison try before he discovered the one that gave off light?* He saved the world from all those unworkable ones. Even if he hadn't succeeded in making a functional bulb, his purpose could simply have been to show us what didn't work.

And becoming a compassionate person means being able to see how other souls are struggling with the reality they've created. And it's fine to give each other help along the way. We are all One in the ultimate form of reality. You're helping yourself.

C: Some channeled books speak of "multiple realities" and "probable realities." Others, including *A Course in Miracles*, say there's only one reality. The rest are illusions. Which do you subscribe to?

F: I know your problem with the word "illusion." It downgrades a person's efforts during incarnations and makes any attempt at knowledge [that's] less than absolute sound like a waste of time. It is not. Anything that contributes Love and Light to a few or to the whole of creation is worthwhile. It shouldn't be denigrated. I agree. I think the philosophies that stress only one reality — God, or Eternity, or a completely harmonious experience of All That Is — want to posit that ideal. It is an ideal. Very few of us are approaching it in our stage of development. If you've reached that ideal, you are the drop fallen back into the wave. As long as you experience yourself as a separate being — incarnate or nonphysical —

you're not there yet. And you continue to create your own reality for better or worse.

C: Can you say more about the word "illusion?"

F: Illusion is a kind of screen like a movie-theater screen. There is no doubt you can see people, objects, action, feel emotion, and so on, from watching a movie screen. It is powerful in a way that can expand consciousness and change behavior. For better or worse.

But you would not confuse the events on a flat screen with your 4-dimensional reality outside the theater. One is more "real" — your reality — than the movie reality. One way to differentiate the two is to call the movie an "illusion" — not in a pejorative way, but in a way that places you outside the movie-screen events.

C: I see. I'm participating in the movie, it's impacting me, but in its illusionary form. I could see monsters on a screen and not be scared of them. You're saying that my everyday life, which seems much more real, can be compared to the illusion of the movie. It has its drama and its comedy and its sequence of events, but it is an illusion compared to your vantage point.

F: Precisely.

C: What would you call your reality? Is it an illusion also?

F: Yes. Anything that still contains separation as in "I'm here, and you're there" is a kind of illusion. Anything less than the full experience of One could be called an illusion. But not to denigrate, only to point out the room to evolve and co-create a version closer to the One.

C: I think I'm learning how to incorporate the greater reality into my daily life in a much more balanced way lately. I can see more through the "greater reality" lens and not get wobbly. It comes more naturally. We are participating/creating all the time. We mostly don't see it, or sometimes we claim credit for something that is a much more collective enterprise.

F: It's all right if the ego claims credit and doesn't see the orchestration. It's when the ego tries to go it alone that it gets into trouble, or runs into its shortcomings.

C: How does evolution connect with co-creation?

F: They are different aspects of the same phenomenon. As we co-create in whatever domain, we evolve our own consciousness as well as the collective consciousness. But evolution does not happen without co-creation. It is all God expanding Self into many more creative forms.

C: Will that process ever stop, or be complete?

F: No, not in the sense of finished product. But the experience of the individual soul will eventually be absorbed into the All That Is. The drop falls back into the wave. The drop no longer has an individual identity. It becomes the *I am the I AM.*

Evolution on "The Other Side"

C: How are you this evening?

F: I'm going through a period of adjustment. When I first arrived in this earth-like dimension, it was startling, yet familiar and comfortable. The colors and sounds were more than I could handle at first. Much to learn, much to enjoy here. I am in this near-earth dimension with many familiar forms and people. Yes, there is architecture and activities that are earth-like. But I could make them disappear for me in a flash. Poof! I keep them, as others here do, for comfort and orientation. I will be able to move on soon (whenever I want) to a dimension of reality with no object projections, just the experience of pure energy and color and sound. Now I know that this is only a port of entry, pleasant as it is. I'm getting ready to move on.

C: I hope that doesn't mean the end of this beautiful relationship.

F: Oh no. I'll be perfectly capable of communicating with you from a higher plane, probably with more clarity and depth. I just need to know that, as a member of a soul group, I'm doing my part to further the Whole. And frankly, I have gotten used to this dimension, wonderful as it is. I'm ready to move into larger dimensions of love and grace and knowledge of the Ferris wheel of possibilities. (I know I've used that image before, but as a child I loved them.)

C: Will you be coming back to earth?

F: I'm enjoying a respite before my next incarnation. A shard of my soul group is still there and I may send another. But a part of me wants to experience other realities — physical, but different. There are many other choices besides Earth for a physical existence.

C: I know. I've put in for a vegan planet already.

F: You'll get a better sense of what's the best scenario for your soul after you arrive here. But I do understand that you don't want to be on a planet that kills and eats other species. But maybe you need to go back to Earth to spread that message?!

C: I guess I could do that, but I'll send a shard* to that vegan planet too.

F: I'm sure you will. You seem determined.

Other Dimensions

C: Are you experiencing other dimensions besides your interpenetrating earth-like one and the physical dimension?

F: Oh, yes, many. We're free to travel to other dimensions — to peek in to higher frequency ones where there aren't structures, only vibrational beings. And we can visit lower realms where we might have someone we'd deeply like to help into the Greater Light.

I have an uncle from the Frances Vaughan life who's in dire straits and I'd like to help him move into more comfort and Love and deeper Communion with All That Is. But he spent much of his life acquiring "things" and traveling all over the world, mainly "consuming" experiences but not absorbing the essence of any. But since his incarnation ended, he's quite depressed about the squalidness of his surroundings. That's what he created while incarnate — something that was missing vital ingredients of Love and co-creation. Of course, his earth home didn't look squalid. It only was squalid in its vibrational level. And so after he died, he moved into a similar [squalid] circumstance. No matter how hard he tries to make it more attractive, the more hollow and tacky it is. [But] he doesn't have to stay there, and I'm trying to send him the message.

C: What do you say?

F: That there are souls waiting to welcome him to a truly beautiful existence with much more Love and Light. All he has to do is recognize his own divinity, the connection to God that he has built in and bingo! He will start to move toward that reality. But as long as he thinks he has to create his reality on his own, that no one loves him, that he's self-sufficient, he will continue to suffer the separation.

The Awareness [of divinity] we're talking about has been lost and found so many times. Lost by individuals, lost by whole cultures, by whole countries. Yet there are always those "keepers of the flame" — or wisdomkeepers as they're known in indigenous cultures — who will be the lamps in the darkness. You are one of them. I was too, in my incarnation, and now I continue from this larger perspective granted to me by the loss of my physical form.

Upheavals: Current and Upcoming

C: This whole planet seems like a pressure cooker to me. Ready to explode at so many different points. Is it as vulnerable as I'm feeling, or am I just tuning into its weaknesses and not its strengths?

F: Both are true. It's agitated, a conundrum of competing forces and overarching problems in many places. Yet there is still a fair amount of "normalcy" where the pressure is barely noticed. People carrying on their lives, businesses coming and going, vacation spots still populated.

C: Is normalcy a consensus reality?

F: Yes and no again. It is being co-created, but it also has a life of its own, so to speak, that's independent of the probable realities being foisted upon it on a daily basis — both hopeful and despairing. Many of them. The negative energies of hatred, greed, and so on attract like-minded energies that might be in the neighborhood.

It's the same on an individual level. Someone putting out energies that are self-serving will attract people with similar energies. If you held the Earth as an individual with a certain unique set of energies, what do you think would be the overall impression to an outsider?

C: I want to think the beauty and caring and creativity and good-heartedness of most of the inhabitants would shine through what might seem like a rough exterior. I don't believe that the overall vibration of earth is hugely deficient.

F: As you well know, Earth is so complex — so many layers, so many individuals past, present, and future who define what this planet's soul looks like — I doubt that even an advanced extraterrestrial could accurately describe its primary chord.

C: I'm remembering a photo that went "viral" on the Internet, which means it showed up on thousands of social media devices around the world. It showed a man, Oscar Alberto Martinez Ramirez and his two-year old daughter Valeria, face down, both drowned, in the Rio Grande River.* They had come all the way from El Salvador and were trying to make it across the border to safety in America. They didn't make it. Somehow the photo captured the mythic quality of what's going on the US southern border: People trying to escape violence and starvation in Central America, and willing to die rather than stay in a place of no hope for survival.

I, and I'm sure many others, sent those two souls loving energies and godspeed as they made their way from this physical dimension to a greater reality.

F: What you did — sending loving energy to someone who needs it. — how powerful that can be. The power of acknowledging the humanity, and the divinity, of each other. [When you try] to erase God from your life, from your day-to-day activities, that is such a mistake. Looking for God in every conceivable activity, finding God in odd places, that's a worthy activity, especially during chaotic times. He/She is there. You just have to ask.

C: People do, in dire situations, and God sometimes fails to show up.

F: That's because people think God is some outside person riding to the rescue. Don't ask for a situation to change. Do whatever you can, even it's only to mitigate some of the pain that's present. Don't keep asking God to do it. Figure out what you can do. You can create miracles if you could tap the god within. That's where your god lives, not on some cloud somewhere.

C: What else can we say to those who want to prepare for changes in our world?

F: You and I are focused on "the greater reality." The message remains the same as in *Book One*: Don't be afraid to die. You live on. Your body returns to the earth. If you have loved ones, younger or older than you, make some provision for their care in case something should happen to you. But be aware that they know what's going on too. In their higher consciousness they see clearly that the world will turn upside down for a while. It will be a terrifying and exhilarating time.

Terrifying because there will be those only concerned with their own survival. Exhilarating because we will all see (I will too) how many humans incarnate today are on hand, ready to jump in, be "first responders" in any ways they can, and be ready to die to make the transition to a more harmonious planet come to fruition.

It's a little like caterpillar-to-butterfly metamorphosis. A caterpillar chugs along. If it's lucky to survive that phase (many don't), then it creates a chrysalis, a cocoon in which a complete transformation takes place.

Entomologists [insect scientists] now know that in the chrysalis there is no form. It's all in embryonic fluid — goo — in which the caterpillar disintegrates and the butterfly begins to form. It's not a direct reshaping of one to another.

It will be difficult for most people to cheer the breakdown period. Only the truly wise (and brave) ones will recognize the necessity and the beauty of the process.

C: Do you foresee that there is a "butterfly" at the end of the chaotic period? A new beauteous form of Earth that could not be predicted from our "caterpillar" form?

F: Yes. Only not everyone will live to enjoy that form. Those who don't will move on to another vantage point. There are many dimensions of existence on this side. Where I am is only my co-creation with others here. But those who can cross the bridge to a greater reality will rejoice in the metamorphosis and take part in the festivals of Light that will take place. We're planning them now.

C: That's a beautiful thought. And from the vantage point outside space/time, they are happening *now*, because everything is concurrent — happening simultaneously.

F: That's right. So we say to those who are hoping and praying for a more loving and balanced planet: "Hold on. It's coming. Maybe not with your present incarnation, but with [your soul's] eyes to see and heart to feel."

EXERCISE: (STEP 3)

Setting up the channel of communication: In this exercise, you will need to ground yourself as well as create an image of a golden antenna reaching into the universe.

There are many ways to ground yourself. Find the one that works best for you. You can imagine you have roots growing down from your feet into the earth, firmly anchored. Another image is of long threads of golden energy originating in your pelvic area and reaching down into the earth where they meet in a golden ball. If you have a mantra you say regularly, such as *Om mani padme hum,** repeating that can be used to ground you. A certain selection of music may work well, or perhaps a recording of environmental sounds such as easy waves on a seashore.

Now you are ready to set up the golden antenna or tube of light that will connect you with your contact. From the top of your head, imagine a golden beam shooting straight up into the sky and beyond. If someone were to be looking from the moon they would see that golden light coming from you and disappearing into the cosmos. Practice this exercise until the image comes easily and you can hold it steadily. Then imagine yourself as a radio receiver, picking up intelligent signals. Finish this sentence: "I am asking for this connection to [*name*] in order to [*fill in purpose*]."

For example, "I Cynthia, am asking for this connection to Frances so that I may better understand the greater reality beyond the space/time dimension."

Again, practice Steps 1, 2, and 3 until they feel comfortable to you.

How can we contact the other side?

The practice of automatic writing

Listen closely for the departed, for they will leave you messages through electrical objects, the natural world, synchronicities, lost and found objects, sudden shattering of glass or picture frames, or well-timed songs on the radio or computer.... Listening is a simple act. Be witness to all the ways our ancestors speak to us through our ears, our hearts, our eyes, our daily lives. Listen so that heaven is heard.

— LISA SMARTT AND MORTON FELIX, *Veil: Love Poems from Across the Threshold*

Early on in our collaboration, Frances told me that there were many "on the other side" who would very much like to contact incarnate loved ones, especially to let them know that after death, they were still "alive." Sometimes an incarnate person doesn't believe that can happen, or doesn't open any channel for the communication to take place, so the discarnate person has to find a way. There are many delightful stories of inexplicable events taking place right at the moment of someone's death to let a loved one know he or she has left. For example, one of my cousins got a cell phone call at 2am that simply left a recorded message with a name from his contact list and the phone number of the person who called. It was my uncle, who was hundreds of miles away. The call registered at the exact minute he died.

Here's another story, given to me by a friend who witnessed it:

Some years ago my mother-in-law arranged to move so that my husband Michael, her son, could be there for her great transition. She was placed in a nursing home in Ukiah where my husband and I could visit her often.

At some point she was transferred to the local hospital because she had suffered a mild stroke. Some days later she had a second and much more serious stroke, which left her brain dead. The decision to unplug her from mechanical support systems was approved by Michael. We sat with her as her breathing became more and more sporadic and finally stopped all together. It was amazingly peaceful. However, it hit Michael hard and he gave into deep, deep tears. The hospital allowed us to stay as long as we wanted, and we sat with her throughout the afternoon.

We drove home in separate cars and as I pulled into the driveway Michael was standing next to his car looking radiant. I was both amazed and curious when he said, "I heard from Mom." He told me that, as he was pulling into the drive, he was having second thoughts and was wondering if he did the right thing by taking her off life-support. At the very moment he had that thought, a sticker that had been put on the inside windshield more than a year before peeled off and fell on the dashboard. It read: "Grateful Dead: Back Stage Pass." This communication was unmistakable in its clarity. Yes, he did do the right thing. His mother's message could not have been more clear.

In this chapter we'll focus on the portal to the greater reality known as *channeling,* or *automatic writing.* Both those terms are used to describe the process of contacting "the other side." Thousands of people have learned how to connect in this way with loved ones who have passed on.

❧

C: Why has channeling become so popular in the last few decades?

F: A playground has different elements to it. Swings, slides, a teeter-totter. We must provide our readers with different ways to approach this material so that they find the right playground amusement. It has to be fun too. I know there are a lot of "upheavals" promised and I don't mean to downplay those. But in order for people to embrace this message, there has to be an attraction. A reason to come forward and move into the greater reality — more than getting over the fear of death. There has to be some day-to-day draw that says, "This will change your life in more ways than one."

We need more incarnate souls as communicators of the greater reality. We must be careful to give proper instructions. But thousands of people channel for themselves and for small groups with no ill effects. Maybe a little wobbliness at first, as you experienced. We in this dimension will be watching over and protecting souls who want to further communication between the living on earth and the souls who have no physicality but who have important messages for [all of] you.

They and other channels become a [Greek]* chorus for this important transition time. It is a crucial epoch-changing time for humanity. You are ready — at least some, and perhaps a majority [of people on earth are ready] — to birth a new form. One that co-creates harmony with each other and the All That Is. But the birthing process is painful and messy, to some extent. We have midwives waiting, souls who have been in training for many lifetimes — including yourself — who will be on hand to help each one make a transition to a new world of expanded consciousness. It's time.

Automatic writing can serve as a conduit to the proper mind states. It can also serve to create the channel bridge to the greater reality in general. To open up, be a portal for those energies to be exchanged between incarnate and non-physical beings of different kinds, not just humans.

That [kind of] communication is an aspect of the greater reality, and is accessible to many people. It can be the direct evidence — the experience that opens the door. You have me as proof. Others can find their partners in automatic writing and make great progress in bringing the wisdom of the other side to bear on individual situations. Have a guide through whatever form works best for [each of] you and use it, perfect it, trust it. It is Intuition personified.

If you want to give it a name or a face or a personage, do it. Nothing wrong with that. Often it will simply be your own higher consciousness, not another entity. But don't try to figure things out with the analytic mind — great for some things, but not the right tool in a situation that has death as its context.

C: So as I understand it, you and I are collaborating using automatic writing. We're suggesting to others to try it, in order to bring information, insight, maybe courage from the other side when needed. If they make contact, is that enough of a breakthrough?

F: No. It's the doorway, but you must go through it, use it yourself, know that it works, and works beautifully when you need it.

C: How does someone do that?

F: You simply learn how to go there easily, with practice, and then start trusting the process for greater insight into many different kinds of situations. Don't get superstitious. What pops up isn't always true, or useful. But allow that channel into your repertoire of responses.

When things get rougher, as they will, that ability to call intuition into play will expand and deepen the responses you can make. You'll be working with a team — your spirit guides, your soul group, discarnates like me who love you and want the best. It's a much bigger team to have than trying to cope on your own. You must be a participating member, a co-creator. You can learn from higher-functioning teams.

Parting the Veil

C: What more can you say about incarnates contacting a loved one who's passed on?

F: Anyone who cares to can open a channel of communication and see if that person "answers the call." Just as you don't always answer the telephone when it rings because you are focused elsewhere, so too a [discarnate] being may be engaged elsewhere. But persistence almost always pays off. You can leave messages on an imaginary answering machine. "I'm trying to reach you. I want to know how you're doing, what you are learning, if you're hurting at all." And so on. Eventually some aspect of the person will answer. Maybe only to say, "I'm doing well. I love you." But a true answer. Always truthful.

C: Can a discarnate being "move on" — what we might call being "out of range"?

F: Yes indeed. As I and many others speaking from this side have indicated, we're evolving in our own ways, and we may have moved away from the physical space/time dimension you're in. In which case, there is still a communication link if both the incarnate and discarnate care about each other and want to make more Love and Light for all involved in the soul group. But if the incarnate is simply trying to carry on a conversation about how things didn't work well, or try to make the discarnate being feel guilty for bad behavior while both were incarnate, it won't work.

The discarnate person has already gone through a life review, and hopefully has experienced the pain caused by his or her misguided behavior. Part of that is asking the injured party to forgive the transgression. [However] the incarnate person may be completely oblivious to the sincere request to forgive.

C: Let's say that in most cases, the request to communicate comes from the highest motivations possible — to reconnect, to express love and to ask for guidance.

F: Then it's up to the discarnate person — a parent, a spouse, or a child who died — to respond with whatever best communication is possible in the situation. Having died and existing in a more Light-filled dimension does not confer omniscience, or profound wisdom. Hardly the case. But there is a more generous, loving omnipresence here — I call it God — that pervades everything and causes each of us to reach for the highest self we can offer.

C: You and I are having a marvelous conversation that we're turning into books. It's ongoing and deep and full of Love and Light, at least for me.

F: And for many others too. That's our purpose — not every [after-death] conversation has publishable material. [smile] We just happen to have that purpose for ours. The great majority of channeled material is simply a conversation between two people who love each other and want to "stay in touch," or, more profoundly, to reach a level of Love that adds to the storehouse of Love we are co-creating with all the others who have tasted the joys of incarnation together.

Good Questions to Ask

C: What are good questions to ask someone on the other side?

F: It's always good to ask how something that's perplexing to you looks from their perspective. You'll always get an answer in a much larger frame than you could devise.

C: I know. You've done that for me many times. What else?

F: Ask what the dimension they're in looks like, or how it's structured, or what's the nature of the activities that go on. Different beings will give you very different answers. Ask the discarnate person whether they're planning their next incarnation. Many are, and have some sense of purpose for it in mind — what they want to learn, and to contribute.

Here's another one: ask the person if they have ever lost their way in the greater reality. Of course, it's not possible to really get lost — there are so many loving souls and spirit guides around to help at a moment's notice. But we can wander off and visit other dimensions, or even other planets with a physical dimension, which can be different than anything we could make sense of. It can be bewildering.

C: I think Bob Monroe* talked about that kind of thing in his books on being out-of-body. He met very strange beings made only of energy frequencies that he had no way to interact with. But he was a brave soul and kept going out for more adventures.

F: He also had many, many lifetimes of explorations, so that new territory wasn't as much of a shock to him as it might be to you and me. He took new kinds of beings in stride, confident in his own inviolate and invulnerable level of development.

C: I hope our readers try the exercises and succeed in making contact. In my experience, they will be rewarded for their efforts in ways they can't imagine. New vistas will open for them. Their fear of death will diminish and they will have the joy of real reunions with loved ones.

F: As well as the assurance that those love bonds endure across dimensions and they will be reunited again.

༄

This piece of poetry was channeled to Lisa Smartt from her father Morton Felix, who had died in 2012.

you are right when you feel me there
you are not imagining or imagined
we are as we were before but I fly in waves of the breezes
in the currents around, above where
the wide windows are —
you my daughter will always be
even when we change again and I am your child

— From the book *Veil* (2018)

༄

C: What can you say about automatic writing situation where you've set the intention of tapping your own higher consciousness? I used to call it "discovering things I didn't know I knew" and write it down in journals.

F: That's an excellent use of the process. As you are finding out, you can ask for specific things, like help on the introduction to our book. Something pops up and it is the perfect idea for the introduction. You often credit me with giving it to you, when in fact it's your own higher consciousness or some other source you tap. When we call these books our "co-creation," they have many more participants than just you and me. Your soul group, my soul group, drawing on experiences each has had or is having through other shards* and their incarnations. We have an enormous library of sources for this material [on our side].

[Speaking of co-creation], you must not hold the book as mostly mine and only partly yours. It is our book, in the same way as if you put flour and eggs and milk together to make a pancake. You can never get the flour or eggs or milk extracted out. They have become one pancake. So this book series is a blend of two sources of consciousness. You could never unbind them into separate ingredients again.

C: OK. It's *our* book.

Limitations on Automatic Writing

C: What are the ways that contacting people on the other side can be helpful to us here?

F: First and foremost, we become more aware that death *is* transition. All the mothers and fathers who have lost children through death, especially sudden death, are comforted when that channel of communication opens and they can have a real conversation. The first message from the other side is, "I love you" and then, "I'm fine. I've made it to the other side, and I'll be fine here waiting for you to join me to be together again. Please carry on your life, knowing I'm here, and will be. There's no rush. Your life will be informed by this loss of me in your world. Learn from it. There's much to learn and I will help."

Other incarnate souls stay in touch with a parent, or a spouse, or other loved one for years, carrying on more and more elaborate conversations, as we are.

C: Besides death as transition, what else can we learn from those communications?

F: The message that Love transcends all boundaries, including space/time, is obvious. Of course, the incarnate one wonders for a long time, "Is this real?" Or, "Am I making this up?" But if you can get past that, the discarnate one can give you signs and wonders that will reinforce the belief — Yes, it is "real" in some sense. It's not "just my imagination." That, by the way, belittles imagination as a tool, but let's discuss that later.

So now one can live a life expanded beyond physical boundaries. The soul has an existence in communication with other souls who don't have bodies. There is such a prohibition in some quarters, especially in the Western world, of talking about such things. There is a need for more people like you, like Regina [C's psychic counselor] to talk openly and naturally about communication from the other side. There's so much to be learned from those who wish to describe things "from the balcony." I certainly did when I passed over the bridge.

I'm now beyond the balcony, so to speak. I've come into my own space of Beauty and Light and will be here as long as I am helpful to you and those who read our books and need help with the "upheavals."

C: What about the gift of seeing everything through a larger frame? I've found that to be most helpful in this collaboration with you. You've reframed tragedy, heroism, even evil to some extent, for me. You've pointed out how what looks like an individual occurrence actually touches the lives of many more people. Like ripples traveling out from a rock thrown into a pool.

F: Yes. Isn't it helpful to see that what we mistook for only a tragic event has ramifications way beyond the death of a single person? Of course, there is the immediate family's loss, but sometimes the way a person dies can galvanize a community like no other event can. [See p. 112 for the Australian mosque story as an example.]

C: Is it possible to contact someone who died "tragically" and find out if they willingly participated in the event?

F: Yes, but for only those close to the person. The choice to die, especially as a young person, is a very personal decision, not open to public inquiry. I don't know of any "victim" who was willing to open up to strangers to tell their story. Perhaps an author could approach such a soul [in order] to write a novel or a play. But it would have to be someone with utmost respect for the soul.

Pitfalls

> *The vast majority of human (as well as other kinds of) spirits reported to be channeled throughout history and especially in the present, come across as benign, loving and helpful. On the whole, the majority of recorded sources appear to be a good deal more spiritually evolved and oriented than most of us, their fellow spirits embodied now on the earth plane.*
>
> —JON KLIMO, author of *Channeling: Investigations on Receiving Information from Paranormal Sources*

C: Are there any pitfalls in the practice of automatic writing that you know of?

F: There are really none to speak of. Even if you contact a negative energy, you can quickly say: "Go away, I do not want to entertain your ugly thoughts. I want more Light to come through this process."

C: I'm sure a few readers will be worried about negative energies. They may not be convinced that just saying "Go away!" will be sufficient.

F: It probably won't be [sufficient] — and they probably won't try automatic writing. I want to assure our readers that attempting to contact people "on the other side" will cause no harm. Not in the sense of negative energies or thoughts taking over their thoughts. However, it's true that a person trying to use automatic writing will encounter some sadness, some grief perhaps, because it rekindles the loss. But the joy that comes with real contact will far surpass any residue of grief. Opening a real channel of communication with a loved one on the other side can be very rich indeed. First of all, the discarnate one is not in a grief mode. The joy of the omnipresent Light and Love of this dimension makes moot the loss of a temporal relationship.

Of course, the discarnate one recognizes the pain of the incarnate one and tries to soothe and assure their loved one that all is well and they will reunite without question. But the first few encounters may trigger the images of [when they were] incarnate together. I can only say that the love they share will be deepened and glorified by the exchanges they have. Love has full reign. Any unresolved issues are set aside, ever blotted out by the glimpse of the next dimension. Trust me, it is so.

C: I do, and I offer it as an answer to our readers' concern about contact.

F: Please remind them also that the [incarnate] person asking for contact has total control of when and how it happens. Total control. We are very respectful of the boundaries that the asking person has, and always honor them.

C: That has certainly been my experience.

F: You can suggest that the person asking for contact make it clear that they want to communicate [in order to provide] the greatest benefit to both sides, and it shall be so.

Boundaries

C: Is the quality of the channeled relationship between an incarnate and a discarnate affected by the relationship they had when they were both incarnate?

F: When we love someone, a person, that person becomes a part of us in a real way. They start to live inside us because, as we've said, we're not physical bodies first and foremost. We're beings of Light and we take in the "beingness" of others, for better or worse, as energy. We invite a part of that person to live inside us — literally, from my vantage point. We grow together at the overlap, whether it be almost total, as in the case of a soulmate, or varying degrees of overlap from great to casual friendships.

[When we co-create relationships] we don't simply allow in the person's energy as they wish. We as individuals invite in those parts of the other person we wish to cultivate within ourselves. That can be anything from the best, most evolved parts, to the tawdry, selfish parts, the ugly parts, like racist or sexist attitudes, because they resonate with ours.

A loving friendship can let in the hurting or self-denying parts, if the receiver cares and has the consciousness to help heal those parts. But the best relationships cultivate and grow the beautiful, gifted, loving parts of each other, and mirror them back to the other person. It happens in a subconscious way, for the most part. We can take on friendships with other people as projects, to help them handle grief or disability. Those are noble ways to serve others. But we must be careful not to make it so lop-sided that the person receiving help always feels one-down, or less than. It must be a sharing of the best parts of each self.

We're always "running into" parts of ourselves inside other people. They are mirrors for us. Do you like what you see? We also run into other souls from our oversoul group and others we've shared friendships or more with, in other lifetimes. You can meet someone and know them or feel such a compatibility that it feels like "we've known each other forever." And maybe you have.

Collaborations with "The Other Side"

C: What about contacting the other side for help on creative endeavors? It's sometimes called *imagination*.

F: We all have "imagination." I do too, much more so than when I was incarnate as Frances Vaughan. The concept of an "imaginal field" is gaining currency in your world. It is a valuable understanding. Say an artist wanted to express an aesthetic — some pain, some trauma — and reached out to the other side for help in expressing it on a canvas.

Several souls on this side might respond with images or designs, or something beyond the scope of the artist. There's a quote from the poet Rumi: *"Out **beyond** ideas of wrongdoing and rightdoing **there is a field**. I'll meet you there. When the soul lies down in that grass the world is too full to talk about."*

That field is the imaginal field where those images, ideas, lines of poetry, melodies, you name it, are transmitted to those who move into the liminal space and ask for help. It's an aspect of the co-creative that we talked about earlier.

We are co-creating all the time, in the seeming reality of space/time as well as here where I am, in a nearby dimension. No one is alone. Lesser and greater beings are affecting your reality all the time with their suggestions, temptations, interesting and novel juxtapositions, and downright bad ideas like [hateful] judgment and violence.

"Listen to your better angels" is an old saying that has much truth.

C: How do we enter that liminal space of the imaginal field?

F: By opening the door, asking to be let in, showing up prepared to accept, be receptive, to open to what shows up. You are always free to reject it, say it's not a fit for you. And you should evaluate anything that comes your way, as you do in other aspects of your life. But if you don't ask, don't seek, don't knock, then you don't receive.

C: What if one tries but is skeptical of getting any results?

F: Depends on who shows up from this side. Chances are nothing will happen for a person who comes with little receptivity. But stories abound about people who were skeptics, but came to believe that psychic abilities are real, for instance.

People may even go on an exploration to disprove something and come out the other side, saying "I was wrong."

John Mack was trained as a doctor and psychiatrist and in 1972 became a professor at Harvard University. Recognized for his outstanding contributions in the field of psychology, in particular, for his writings on suicidal patients, and on heroin addiction, Mack was appointed head of Psychiatry at Harvard Medical School in 1977. In the early 1990s, he initiated a study of 200 people who claimed to have been abducted by aliens. He wanted to find out what sort of mental illness was afflicting these people.

By 1994, he was no longer saying that he thought stories of abduction were hallucinations. In an interview on the BBC, Mack was quoted as saying, "I would never say, yes, there are aliens taking people. I would say there is a compelling powerful phenomenon here that I can't account for in any other way, that's mysterious. Yet I can't know what it is, but it seems to me that it invites a deeper, further inquiry."

Harvard formed a committee to try to expel the tenured professor, but many came to his defense, and Harvard reaffirmed Dr. Mack's "academic freedom to study what he wished and to state his opinions without impediment." In his book, Passport to the Cosmos: Human Transformation and Alien Encounters (1999), Mack came to label the stories as "visionary encounters."

[See **Book References** for John Mack's two books on his research on "alien abduction"]

C: Anything else you can say about the benefits of being open to contact with the other side?

F: Contact with those "on the other side" — "the dead" — is only a small step into the greater reality. But it is a huge one in terms of breaking the taboo on knowing there is so much more than the space/time dimension. Reality is so much more grand, more complex, and infinitely expanding. As the Chinese saying goes: "A journey of a thousand miles begins with a single step." That single step for our readers could very well be communication with a loved one who is enjoying the greater reality.

EXERCISE: (STEP 4)

Protection for crossing into the channeling process: Know that higher-level guides and contacts have your well-being as their main concern. At this step in the process, you'll make sure that you are connecting to the entity you've asked for, or a being who will be a source of guidance and clarity for your highest self.

After you have practiced the Steps 1, 2, and 3, you are ready to "knock on the door." But first ask your own spirit guides for protection from any negative energies. Here is part of the affirmation used by students at the Monroe Institute* when they are working on out-of-body exercises:

I deeply desire the assistance of those individuals whose wisdom, development, and experience are equal to or greater than my own. I ask their guidance and protection from any influence or any source that might provide me with less than my stated desires.

It will be useful to memorize the protection request so you can say it as needed, and confidently.

What are we here to learn?

~~✒~~

The human heart can go the lengths of God...
Dark and cold we may be, but this
Is no winter now. The frozen misery
Of centuries breaks, cracks, begins to move;
The thunder is the thunder of the floes,
The thaw, the flood, the upstart Spring.

Thank God our time is now when wrong
Comes up to face us everywhere.
Never to leave us till we take
The longest stride of soul we ever took.

Affairs are now soul size.
The enterprise
Is exploration into God.
Where are you making for? It takes
So many thousand years to wake,
But will you wake for pity's sake!

— CHRISTOPHER FRY (English poet and playwright)
excerpt from "A Sleep of Prisoners"

Having a sense of purpose *before* you incarnate on earth is probably a concept new to most readers. We will further explore this theme in *Seven Questions, Book Three*. But suffice it for now simply to be open to the possibility. Each individual soul comes with a purpose to learn something new, or continue to develop a talent begun in a prior lifetime.

Mozart is often mentioned as a case in point. At the age of five, he was competent enough at piano and violin to create new compositions and to perform before European royalty. By the age of thirteen, Srinivasa Ramanujan, an Indian mathematician, was generating his own theorems in number theory that he called "God's thoughts." When he was 27, Ramanujan was invited to Cambridge University in England, where his genius was recognized. He became the first person of Indian descent elected to be a Fellow of Trinity College Cambridge.

Most of us come into an incarnation with more modest goals, but they always have to do with learning something that benefits the Whole. Imagine if we came in knowing everything! There would be nothing left to learn, no desire to explore, no reason to reincarnate.

~⊚

C: Frances, what are we here to learn during an incarnation on earth?

F: The larger or deeper question that comes to me is: "What is the knowledge that each of us seeks that is soul-deep?" Not just interesting knowledge about humans and our condition and why we're here. A soul incarnates because it wants to. No one forces it. That's a decision entirely made by the soul's group — to send a shard of itself to incarnate on earth to gain knowledge for the whole group.

You might ask: "Why not send the whole soul group?" For some soul groups, there is a version of that. Families choose to incarnate together and take different roles in each lifetime or incarnation. When you spend many lifetimes with the same shards — all of one soul, mind you — you get to know the character of that soul very deeply. Whatever pieces don't quite fit together learn to do so.

Another model is the single shard, supported by the soul group in the Home dimension. They're rooting for that piece of the Whole to succeed.

Don't forget that an earth incarnation is a particularly arduous journey. Other planes of existence offer easier accommodations. Why does someone on earth choose mountain climbing, or trying to win a Nobel prize? Because it's hard and the rewards are plentiful. Not just earthly recognition but also a sense of evolution for the soul. That's what it's about.

C: Can you say more about soul evolution? We understand evolution here on earth as better adaptation, more survival power, more intelligence, more resilience, more awareness — and in some species — more beauty.

F: All that and more. Much more. We are adding to God's splendor, to the splendor of the space/time universe as well as to the dimensions of eternity. It's co-creation again. Learning how to cooperate, to harmonize, to become each other, because we are, after all, all One. It's all *a journey to the One.*

Along the way, we each create our own unique version of a self. Then we collaborate in small, then large, groups. Then we merge into a greater entity that contains much more perspective and knowledge of the Whole, as Seth demonstrates in the Jane Roberts books.

> *When you enter time and physical life, you are already aware of its conditions. You are biologically and psychologically predisposed to grow within that rich environment, to contribute on all levels to the fulfillment of your species — but more than this, to add your own unique viewpoint and experience to the greater patterns of consciousness of which you are a part.*
>
> — JANE ROBERTS/SETH, *The Individual and the Nature of Mass Events*

F: Much of what Seth teaches is way beyond our capacity (mine too) of truly grasping because of his stage of evolution. He's adept at words. Some advanced souls use art forms, or symbols, or rituals in order to teach us the greater dimensions of God. Words are a bit archaic. It takes so many to get new ideas across to a general audience. But a magnificent sunset, a cloud formation within a setting sun — purples and hues of orange — it takes your breath away. That's art teaching us, giving us a glimpse, like a near-death experience, of the utter shattering of our narrow categories.

Love Is All You Need

F: Also, Earth provides a splendid setting for Love of all kinds — mother's love, spousal love, love of fellow species, and love of life itself. A few fortunate people allow themselves to fall in love with Life as it manifests in all its diversity. And even beyond that, one can find Aliveness in other emotional areas — wars, emergency rooms, and in solitary confinement. Yes, even there.

There is a spiritual practice in eastern religions of someone living in a cave for years at a time. People honor such a person by bringing him or her food and other necessities. Being in solitary confinement has many of the same aspects. You generally have to commit an act that society finds abhorrent, and perhaps it was.

It's not common, but it happens that such a person finds God in the prison cell. Not a journey one necessarily plans, but arrives at nevertheless.

C: So many routes to the All That Is.

F: There is no such thing as a solo incarnation. First you pick your parents — or, I should say, the sperm and egg donors for your incarnation. Occasionally you never learn who one or both are. But all the circumstances of that entry were seen and agreed upon by the participant.

C: What happens when a fetus is aborted?

F: A soul dies, but only temporarily. Souls are inviolate and cannot be destroyed. The soul was about to make an entry, but the body was aborted. The soul may be disappointed but will try again soon to find a suitable situation for an incarnation that promises to provide the learning it's looking for.

Sometimes the circumstances of the mother or both parents is such that the purpose the soul had in this incarnation would have been very difficult or impossible to achieve. Nothing lost. Only some time and space on earth. We all have many lifetimes.

C: What are you engaged in during this stay in the near-earth dimension?

F: Still the same concern about the current upheavals. Still wanting to provide information, such as "Death is a transition," but beyond that I'm finding ways to open the magnificence of my existence to others who are ready to enter it. I don't mean they are about to die. But having this near-ecstasy experience can help frame the whole experience of upheavals and encountering the mix of emotions and demands on the psyche to maintain Love as best it can be held in a time of chaos.

Only a few saints, "advanced beings," will show up during those times. They are now in the places where chaos is already setting in. More are on the horizon, or in the clouds, so to speak. They will provide direction and comfort. But most people will stay the course as long as they are able, and then let go and cross the bridge. You will be one of those. And you will know you've done a fine job of preparing yourself and many others for this time of planetary rebalance.

C: I suspect you'd be one of the saints if you were still around.

F: I doubt it. I'm in a good place in my sense of my soul's evolution, but having the wherewithal to lead people out of fear and into love when everything is crumbling is a tall task. I did what I could in teaching "Live from Love, not from fear." Not in big public ways but in my own chosen modes.

C: You did a beautiful job. So many people are indebted to you for your wisdom and kindness, as well as your books and teachings. And then there are your therapy patients — the many lives you touched and continue to do so through this collaboration with me. You have given many blessings.

F: And received back 100-fold.

Each Incarnation Teaches Love

C: Can you say something more specific about why we incarnate on earth? What are we here to learn, besides the deepening of moral values?

F: For those of us who choose to incarnate on earth — and I'll be returning shortly, in one of my soul group shards — the physical density of an earth existence is such a contrast to the finer energy-being I am right now. It reminds us that there are so many forms of God's creations. We know that from looking at all the different insects, fish, mammals on earth. And those are only the ones who co-exist with us while we're there. Hundreds of thousands more forms have come and gone.

The myriad forms beg us to consider what creativity is possible and what we [can do] as co-creators not only of our own consciousness — but also the consciousness of the Whole Universe. Each earth incarnation is a message of the potential of creative consciousness without limit. That's one learning.

Another is the particular challenge of living then dying, when our greater selves know there's no such thing as death. But existence takes many forms. A human body is only one, but how we love it when we have one. Learning how to take care of this beautiful creation from our mother, father and ancestors is a sacred responsibility. Neglecting it is an affront to the whole species. Overindulging it is also a transgression of its purpose to carry us through our lives, however long or short they are. Balance, always balance. The oscillation of yin and yang.

And of course, the final test of having a body — can you let go when its purpose as your vehicle in that dimension has been fulfilled? Or do you choose to try to hold onto it with all manner of interventions and costs?

It's tough to be born. It's tough to die. Maybe I should say it's a lesson in commitment while you have it [life], and a final exam to see if you've learned to let it go because it's not who you really are. And you've discovered that along the way. Advanced souls who still incarnate are able to glide in and out more gracefully.

C: You seemed to do that. I saw you — we had dinner together with our spouses and other friends — and a week later you died.

F: I did my best, and yes I did have a greater understanding of the process of making my way out.

C: That's a marvelous thing to think about — simply being here to learn impermanence, as the Buddhists say. Or more correctly, to learn what is impermanent and what is eternal.

F: People at the highest level of attainment of that knowledge while incarnate are the ones who volunteer for dangerous assignments. Or who take risks in dangerous sports or careers like fire fighters.

C: I get an image of those people who put a tightrope across Niagara Falls and walk across holding a balancing pole. It seems utterly impossible, but a few people do it.

F: They are able to do it because they know that the body is not who they are. Whatever happens, they will be fine. People who are afraid to die, who don't know, deep down, that there is life after life, would never make it. It's a kind of psychic ability, but only for a rare few individuals.

How Does Hatred Enter This Reality?

C: I have a question that may or may not be pertinent: Why do some people become depraved? So angry that they shoot to kill innocent people, or purposely run into them with a vehicle? It seems like such a deep-seated hatred, so unbelievably cruel and hurtful.

F: You're putting your finger on part of it. Those individuals put their lives into a vortex of hatred and lies, and imagine everything is against them. It goes deeper and deeper into their minds. Just as we have said that we have the power to produce miracles, we can also tap that energy to do extraordinary damage.

C: But why does it turn so ugly?

F: Because there is no Light there. All is dark, menacing, foreboding and hate-filled. No Light. A complete rejection of God, of Life, of the Communion of souls we all belong to.

C: I still don't understand what drives some people in that direction.

F: A survival instinct that says "I must kill or be killed. Die. But not before my life means something — I will break the rules so grossly that I will be known as a hero to others who wish to break the rules but 'don't have the guts' to do it." They say, "Let's blow it all up. There's no reason for anything to exist. There is nothing in this world worth living for. I will find an easy target — people worshipping in their sacred place, and show them how stupid that is. Someone as little as me can cause great damage and a huge amount of suffering. I can do it. I *will* do it."

C: Can we do anything to stop these outrages? They happen almost every day now.

F: It's all part of the pressure being exerted on all systems. The fragility of some of the institutions is being revealed. A single person can bring down a community. What power!

C: But what often happens is the community wakes up to its Communion, its Love, and becomes stronger. Other people outside the community that's affected rush in to help. The horrible act actually has the opposite effect.

F: Precisely. And in a larger-frame way of looking at why events happen, that is a feature of it. Certainly not the intent of the perpetrator, nor is it "God's will" in some perverse sense. It is a human being pushed to a brink of absolute despair and acting out before they die or get incarcerated for the rest of their lives.

We are Love. All of us, each of us, contain the spark of divinity within us, and to act in such a terrible manner is a stab (in a figurative sense) to the soul. It will take many lifetimes and much healing energy from helpers to get past the wounds of those deeds. Those people deserve our compassion. Of course, the actions are horrific. But as Jesus said, "Love the sinner, hate the sin." We've barely begun as a species to practice that. Hate and condemnation are so much easier.

C: If we plan our incarnations to learn something that expands our individual consciousness as well as that of our group soul, how do you explain that some people end up with lives full of hatred for others, and who commit abominable acts of violence and cruelty towards others? Is that built into the life plan before birth?

F: No. Of course not. We don't incarnate to learn hatred or how to harm others in insidious ways. People who get stuck in those deep dark wells of separation from others, sometimes all others, have been treated very badly early in that lifetime, and maybe in others as well. As we've said earlier, you come in with your game plan and choose your parents and circumstances. But then you have a setting with variables or factors you didn't choose and you have to carry out your purpose, learn what you came to learn.

There are people, places and situations that can challenge you to a level [of hatred or violence]. To maintain yourself as a divine presence while incarnate is the point. And there are degrees of separation from the Source of Love and Consciousness that are so ugly that it tests your ability to survive or die [trying]. Or [you could choose to] succumb to the temptation to go in that direction because it seems easier in the moment.

Make no mistake about it, the universe is filled with myriad experiments in form and consciousness. Some have gone terribly wrong and will extinct themselves, while the souls involved move on, get care and are healed. The healing energies, coming from love and communion, are very powerful. So are the separation energies. Why they exist in the first place is another topic, not for tonight.

[C: During this session with Frances, I had an experience without words of being taken into the entrance to hell — so frightening, so immensely unbearable that I was frozen. "I cannot proceed" was what I was finally able to send as a thought form to Frances. Then it all vanished. I realized I was being shown how dark the dark place was, and I was unable to take any step in that direction]

C: I'm still not seeing the source of the individual's malaise or disease or whatever it is. I'm thinking that some sort of horrible condition in childhood pushed them. But many people with similar circumstances don't go off like that.

F: Let's use an analogy from our *Portals* section. We suggested in *Book One* that there are portals to a direct experience of the greater reality. We said you could try various things like cultivating psychic abilities, or going deeply into art or music, or following a meditation tradition. So a person can take a step or two in that direction and find out that there is something larger going on beyond material space/time realities. And with the intention of deepening your love for others, your sense of the Communion with the All that is, you'll be rewarded with an experience that changes your life for the better and lessens your fear of death.

What if you enter a portal with a basically hostile attitude? You've found yourself in a dead-end job, or in a relationship that emphasizes the worst aspects of both people, not the best. And so on. You enter a portal and find that the power of Love that others find is based on their intention. The Greater Reality beyond the portal is simply greater than ordinary reality. You can increase your power to do harm, lessen your fear of death to the point of becoming a suicide bomber, and go out and kill many people at once. The consensus rules are suspended. You become what used to be called a devil, or a misanthrope, but now often is called a terrorist.

C: Will our book open doors for that kind of person too?

F: I doubt that "that kind of person" will pick up and read our books. But that could happen. They are more often on the Internet, looking for the dark corners where people with similar thoughts congregate. That deepens and strengthens their resolve to break the rules.

A Swing Into The Greater Reality

C: To take another step into what an incarnation can teach us, let's return to a further exploration of *I am the I AM*.

F: It's the acknowledgment that you *are* divine. You are part of the Great Divinity that is all, that is Infinite, Eternal and exists everywhere at once. That's way too big and scary for most people. It's much easier to be small — a grain of sand. Then you're a manageable size. Not something so important whose every thought comes to fruition somewhere. Way too much responsibility! [smile]

I don't mean that as an ego statement. The ego of some people could easily latch onto a sense of self-importance. But the ego sees itself as an individual [who is] being great. The kind of perception contained in the "I am the I Am" is all about accepting our participation in a greater consciousness, the greater reality, the Godhead. No words capture it and some are tainted with cultural baggage.

I am the I AM is the mantra of a fully realized, fully participating soul in as wide a berth of awareness as one has access to. Rather than clinging to a smaller sense of your self, it's a letting go. Imagine swinging on a swing at a park. It's big swing with long chains so that you can fly out ten feet or more forward and backward. What freedom, what fun. What happens if you get scared? You can get in trouble if you try to slow down too fast. The "I am the I AM" is letting the swing take you — out into the stars, into the Milky Way. And if you pull the chains you hold onto and stretch your legs as you come forward, you can go higher and higher. Remember that feeling?

The swing in the greater reality playground has no limits. You can't get hurt. But you can decide that you're not worthy to go higher, or you're not ready. That's fine. Just know that you'll keep discovering you *can* go higher and higher as you cycle through various lifetimes. And then there's the moment when you realize you don't *have* to slow down, that is, reincarnate on earth or take on a form in some other physical system.

You're free to move on to somewhere I can't yet describe but I know exists for me and for every other person reading this material. You can count on it, and it is counting on you to participate when you're ready.

C: What's the "it?"

F: God, Oneness, the Ocean of Love. Pick your favorite label. It's an experience, not something that the intellect can grab. No words, just pure bliss. I get glimpses of it. I can't let the swing go higher and higher without feeling a little nervous too. I'm learning, as we all are. One day [smile at space/time reference] that part of our education as individuals will be over. Enjoy it, learn from it while you can. It's only a small part of what is and what you are.

> *"Our deepest fear is not that we are inadequate. Our deepest fear is that we are powerful beyond measure. It is our light, not our darkness that most frightens us.... Your playing small does not serve the world. There is nothing enlightened about shrinking so that other people won't feel insecure around you. We are all meant to shine, as children do. We were born to make manifest*

the glory of God that is within us. It's not just in some of us; it's in everyone. And as we let our own light shine, we unconsciously give other people permission to do the same. As we are liberated from our own fear, our presence automatically liberates others."

—Marianne Williamson, author, speaker, presidential candidate in 2020

Learning to Reject No One

[Note from Cynthia: My time with Frances since we began our sessions in January, 2018, has been one of expansion of my mind and heart. Here's an example.]

The Half-Naked Man and the Turkeys

As I was pulling up to the curb to park near a bakery, I noticed a half-naked man pushing a shopping cart full of his belongings along the sidewalk. In 50 degree weather, he had no shirt. And probably no home. I walked slowly along the sidewalk behind him as I made my way to the bakery. (The irony was not lost on me.) While I was waiting in line in the busy store, I looked out the window and saw a small group of wild turkeys, three or four, gathered at the curb of the four-lane main thoroughfare. It was busy at that time of the morning and they were trying to cross the street. Wild turkeys have taken up residence in the neighborhoods of the East Bay in an uneasy co-existence with the human inhabitants.

I bought my pastries and as I came outside I saw the half-naked man standing in the middle of the street, stopping traffic in both directions. The turkeys were crossing the street to the other side. Could I have done that? No. Why did he do that? I cannot say. I just knew this was a perfect example of the Hindu saying: This is my guru in a distressing disguise.

∼◎

C: Frances, what have you learned recently that you can share?

F: Love is the answer, but it's also the question. What is it? What does it look like? What colors is it? We must get beyond romantic love. Sometimes love is only recognized by its absence. Losing a child who dies from cancer creates such a hole in the psyche, in the heart. Losing a beautiful vista to oil rigs, or a forest fire, or a bulldozer. The heartache of that loss tells us something about the power of love and what it really looks and feels like when it predominates your consciousness. Cultivating love on a daily basis — big things like helping a friend in a tough situation, little things like making a special meal for someone that says "I love you."

C: The digital age that we are in seems to isolate people in their individual realities — in their cell phones. Are the younger generations learning to know what love is?

F: Of course they do. The presence of Love in our souls is a given. But it can be buried by materialism and addiction to novelty, too much entertainment, like too much chocolate, or too much TV.

C: What brings a person back to their souls — to the love that always resides there, to our connection to the divine?

F: Sometimes one must hit bottom — a place where it's so dark that it feels Love doesn't exist. Then a kind word, a touch, a recognition of one's divinity from a person who knows the value of that, is all that's necessary.

Sometimes a person is so scarred, so damaged by a difficult lifetime, that the reclamation project can take several lifetimes to heal, to convince the soul that the presence of *All That Is* **is** the reality we all crave and participate in. I can't say this more strongly: NO ONE is ever lost forever. NO ONE is abandoned, no matter how much "evil" they've committed. I think if we accept that, we go a long way toward bringing the Light and Love of God's presence to a single soul, because we don't reject anyone despite their bad behavior.

C: That reminds me of a beautiful woman I worked with during my audio career. Her name was Virginia Satir. She was a family therapist who worked with the "rejects' of the world. There was one story about when she worked with a teenager who had killed both his parents. She talked to him with compassion and forgiveness. He was punished for his crimes, but I can't help but think that his soul was touched and opened up by her kindness. How bad must things be to kill your parents? I don't know the circumstances, but I imagine that the self-hatred was as deep as the hatred toward the parents.

F: I believe so. I know of Virginia Satir. She was a legend in her own time. She gave herself to people in very difficult situations, to people most others would look down on, or despise. You can consider some behavior morally repugnant, but if you remember that there is a soul within a very distressed or diseased mind, you can find the divine. It takes special people, like Virginia Satir, to be able to see the Light within such a person. I wish we all had that capability. We despise those things in others we are afraid might lurk within ourselves. It's an old cliché, but true.

> *I want to love you without clutching, appreciate you without judging, join you without invading, invite you without demanding, leave you without guilt, criticize you without blaming, and help you without insulting. If I can have the same from you, then we can truly meet and enrich each other.* — VIRGINIA SATIR

....

EXERCISE: (STEP 5)

Setting your intention: Finish this sentence: "I am asking for this connection to [name] in order to [ ]."

> *For example, "I, Cynthia, am asking for this connection to Frances so that I may better understand the greater reality beyond the space/time dimension."*

At this step in the process, we're making sure that you will be connected to the entity you've asked for, or a being who will be a source of guidance and clarity for your highest self. Practice Steps 1 through 5 until you are very comfortable with the process.

....

How do we live our purpose during the upheavals?

≈

The purpose of life is to obey the hidden command which ensures harmony among all and creates an ever better world. We are not created only to enjoy the world, we are created in order to evolve the cosmos.

— MARIA MONTESSORI, physician and philosopher of education (1870-1952)

Let's move into the heart of the upheavals: How do we live our purpose during these times?

In a word, we keep our eyes on the *prize*. We each arrive as a seed to flourish, or not, during a lifetime. The belief of the mind, the desire of the heart, when intertwined, drive us toward the Holy Grail of the ripened soul. There is the *telos* of becoming, some deep knowing that our purpose is to become a unique aspect of the Divine Whole. That purpose drives us to develop at each stage of our lives, to explore and create.

Staying true to that quest is challenging enough in so-called "normal" times. How much more difficult is it during times where terms such as *climate chaos, extinction, the rise of autocrats* and *the end of civilization as we know it* are heard more frequently? Even if you feel you have a good grasp of your purpose at this point in your life, how strongly can you hold onto it as the storms of change and rebalance engulf us?

Let's explore with Frances how each of us can hold on during the upheavals.

><©

C: Let's return to the concept that may be new for our readers: we come into an incarnation with a life purpose. Can you say more about that in the context of current upheavals?

F: Life purpose goes with a lifetime. Each lifetime that a soul chooses to manifest [incarnate] has a primary lesson or learning.

C: Can you give me an example?

F: [A person says] I want to be known for my ability in a certain field — math or teaching children in kindergarten, or having beautiful dogs, or leading a contemplative life. There are as many unique life purposes as there are souls, so no two life purposes are identical. But the exterior — or the visible aspects of one's life purpose — is not the goal. The goal lies deeper in the being of the person. In order to exhibit the trait you desire, the skill, the value you want to stand for, you must prepare the inner field that produces the fruit of the goal — the visible part. But so much thought and energy and Love must be the basis for the unfolding. There is no such thing as a manifestation of purpose without a large energetic coordination of elements that create it.

C: How do you choose beforehand? You and others have said that a life purpose is chosen before birth and then you look for the best parents and life circumstances within which to make it "manifest."

F: And don't forget all the effort put into gestating yourself in the womb, and then negotiating the huge challenges of space/time before you get yourself to the point of manifesting your contribution. The best purposes, so to speak, are always about contribution, service to the Whole. Otherwise why bother? Individualized goals may benefit a few. But Love is always involved in the purpose, or more specifically, finding out how we each are connected to the whole of existence.

A light bulb has a purpose — to give light. Your purpose can be as simple as that: "I came here during this incarnation to shine a light on this aspect of physical reality — the art form, or vista, or this problem, or cause — my vision of a better world."

Everyone is a light bulb in that sense, yet only the really bright ones or obnoxious ones get the attention. One of the ways we evolve as spiritual beings is to see the "lightbulbness" of each individual.

C: I think you can see almost everyone's if you simply stop and look carefully. Be it the clerk at the grocery store or the guy up on a ladder fixing the telephone wires. Having that as an exercise — looking for each other's light — seems to me to be a purpose unto itself.

F: It is. A noble one. [Our mutual friend] Angie Arrien* had that one at genius level when she was incarnate. When someone came to her with an idea, or something they felt strongly about, she saw the "light" within it, the flame of creation, and blew on it to fan it into a higher flame. People so loved her and her enthusiasm. She fanned many flames into a drive to complete the vision the individual saw. She kindled [the light bulb in] them.

C: I know. I was one of those people. She and I combined my contribution of wisdom circles with her material on the Four-Fold Way, and together created a beautiful set of CDs that touched many people.

F: That's a fine example of coming into an incarnation with a purpose — to kindle the hearts and minds of others to exceed their expectations of themselves. Angie could do that. That was her gift and her purpose.

C: What if your purpose is to point out that the ways we've constructed our reality are often unfair to people of color, or people with disabilities, or people whose gender doesn't fit a neat label?

F: You can choose to do that by being one of those who's finding your soul and making those connections with and for others. It's a beautiful challenge — to realize that the physical look is a trapping, a costume. Sometimes you're challenged to find the guru in "disguise." It's so much easier to take the superficial as the essence. You must do your homework, your spiritual homework to recognize another person's essential being. Also, trying to figure out their life purpose is a noble act, an act of lovingkindness for you [that benefits you] as well as that guru in disguise.

Knowing Our Unique Purpose

C: Please say more about finding our unique purpose.

F: It has to involve creativity. Doing something uniquely your own.

Raising a child or children is always a unique experiment and challenge. But for many of us the purpose has to do with recognizing that we are truly co-creators of everything we see. It is a "consensus reality" in ways we can hardly imagine.

Let's start with a small, simple example. A household with two adults and two children. Every single instance where that configuration exists on the planet is unique. No two alike. Each being brings his or her own purpose, challenges from a health standpoint, level of intelligence, and personality to the family group. Each one of the individuals has already agreed in advance (before birth) to participate in this grouping, and has some sense of what the dramas and joys are going to be. Then it's up to the four of them to co-create the best possible scenario for the love and learning to happen.

Another example would be a zoo where having all these different animals in one place causes problems for each animal. The gazelle knows there's a lion nearby. The exotic birds know they can't escape. So they have to co-create as harmonious a situation as possible. It's "unnatural" or artificial, for sure. But it's their lot in this lifetime so they try to figure out how to make it work.

C: What about the young woman who was an intern with the zoo where a lion got out and killed her?

F: It was her choice to be there with those animals she loved. She knew how dangerous it was. I don't know the specifics, but she could have decided that being killed by a lion was an exciting way to end her life. Or she could have been incredibly naïve about the behavior of such beasts. In any event, she learned a strong lesson about life on earth and may come back in another lifetime as a tamer of lions, or maybe live in an African village with lions nearby and learn how to truly live with them, as the Bushmen do.

There's always a larger frame we can put on an event or a situation to see the learning that's supposed to take place. Let me emphasize that it doesn't always happen — that the lesson is learned. Sometimes a person can walk away from just the situation that would give them what they're hoping for. Yet with free will, they choose to go in a different direction, or avoid the challenge. Happens all the time.

C: Can you say more about life purpose? How do we come to know what it is?

F: I doubt that most people are consciously aware of their purpose for an incarnation. It is properly defined before birth. But then you're born into a situation with variables other than the ones you planned on. That's what *co*-creation is all about. It's *co*. Collaborative, as this book is.

When challenges arise, that's the stuff of learning. And what creative pieces you can design to address the unknowns. Remember that the purpose does not have to be grand, or recognized, or even mentioned by anyone else. It's your purpose, and it could be as simple as surviving in very difficult circumstances, or building an organization that helps the homeless, or creating a unique piece of art from old scraps of things. It doesn't really matter what the outcome is. You can "fail" at trying something, and that can be the "learning" — exactly what your purpose was in trying it.

C: One of my favorite examples is told by J. K. Rowling, the author of the Harry Potter book series. She wrote the first book and went through at least a dozen rejections from agents and publishers before she got a modest advance from a British publisher. When the seventh book in the series came out in 2007, it sold 11 million copies in the first 24 hours.

Finding Our Purpose in Difficult Times

C: What else would you like to tell us today?

F: Imagine a mosaic tile wall stretching in right and left directions, with no ends in sight, filled with sparkling, colored tiles that look like jewels. That's what each person, each plant, each ant or butterfly is — a beautiful mosaic that's alive, pulsating with Light and humming with God's music.

You must not cast out any piece, even the ones that seem shabby, or have bad intent. The more you and all of us can embrace the fact that the Universe is a Whole, nothing can be thrown out. We can only help, and pray for and support those who need extra help.

[Incarnate humans] are holding the tension of opposites — the world of physical and space/time realities is wobbling badly. So much dissension and suffering, and deaths of noble ones who are trying to draw our attention to major injustices. The way of hatred and division is a dead-end. That will shortly be more clear.

The tendency of things to fall apart is being met by the strong sense of pulling together, the need for community, and most of all, for a clarity of higher values and a vision of how to achieve those values in the next iteration of life on earth.

I'm here to help you articulate those values. But most important, as we've said in *Book One*, is the freedom to act because there is no death. No need to be afraid of dying. The dying time may be difficult; it most often is, no matter how "saintly" you are.

But the thrust of the innate consciousness you share with a much larger universe of beings is the promise of life after life that will come true after your purpose is accomplished as best as you can carry it out [on earth].

C: What guidelines can we use during this difficult time?

F: It depends on what your "present moment" looks like. Is it about [physical] survival? Taking care of someone who needs you? Making a contribution to an organization whose values you want to promote? Being a good farmer? A good cook making nurturing food for others?

Each act is a small tile in the mosaic. But get that piece under a microscope (which God does) and it reveals worlds of color, of depth and atoms swirling with cosmic energy. God is the all-pervasive, the all-knowing, loving presence of the sum of everything.

One promise I can make is that the suffering will end for the individual soul who enters into this greater reality with "eyes open," so to speak. With the anticipation of love and rest awaiting. It's going to be hard for so many. Just know that great upheavals have happened before, and will happen again.

Staying the Course

F: Hello, dear one. How are you?

C: A bit wobbly lately. Not sure if some of the dire messages/ dreams I'm having are the result of my own paranoia, or messages from "at large."

F: You know they are not strictly your own. The newspapers, the media are full of dire events, warnings of catastrophe on the horizon.

C: But I wonder if I'm magnifying them through my fears.

F: No, you're not. You're simply tuning in to the level you can handle — more than most, not as much as some. We must proceed to let those who want to know how to cope with the Current Upheavals can best prepare themselves. Our books are a small but significant part of the picture. Let's continue with our work.

C: All right. What's the best level from which to view all the crumbling infrastructure, all the challenges we face?

F: From the ground level — from the perspective of your own life, your family and loved ones. There are [also] those who are devoted to larger frames — homeless shelters, national security, the functioning electricity grid. Each of you has a grounding point, and participation in larger structures too. Plus you can support the larger enterprises with your love and energy, and even with a check [donation] once in a while.

What matters is your outlook on what is happening and what roles you want to play as the cycle of this civilization finishes its completed circle. Changing that [trajectory] is not something you can do. But guiding it by infusing Love and Light into every possible event and situation is something each person can do. (Me too)

That's not the same as generous people who allow themselves to be martyred to bring attention [to a cause]. Like the Muslim worshippers in New Zealand whose house of worship was entered by someone whose only recourse, as he saw it, was to kill many Muslims who he thought were causing his pain. He was wrong, of course. They were victims of the same craziness that afflicted him. But they were willing, albeit not joyfully, not without their own deep pain at leaving their families and loved ones, but willing to be martyrs to the hatred that's been targeted at them. Look at the response: a huge outpouring of grief and support from other religious congregations to offer them comfort and solidarity in their utter pain.

How many lives were touched and permanently changed by that event? Many more than the number of people who died in that mosque. That horrible event became a touchstone of Awareness for so many more to understand and embrace the survivors as "fellow beings," not "other" people they had no kinship with.

≈

On March 15, 2019, a man opened fire in a Muslim mosque in Christchurch, New Zealand, and livestreamed the event on his Facebook page. After the 6-minute attack at Al Nour mosque, the shooter moved to Linwood Islamic Center nearby and shot more defenseless people outside the building. Abdul Aziz Wahabzadaat, a worshipper at Linwood, heard the shots, ran outside and tried to distract the shooter by shouting "I'm here. I'm here." He was shot by the gunman and wounded. At the end of the episode, 51 people were dead and 49 injured. The incident was seen by millions of people on Facebook and YouTube until it was taken off the Internet. A week later, over 20,000 people, representing a variety of faiths, attended a memorial. Funds were set up in New Zealand and around the world to support the victims' families. Over 10 million dollars was raised within weeks. The shooter was charged with 51 counts of murder and pleaded not guilty. His trial was scheduled for May, 2020.

❧

C: How else can we expand our Awareness, in addition to witnessing and responding to such a huge tragedy for that Muslim community?

F: Awareness grows in little ways and big ways. The Awareness of what's taking place on Planet Earth right now is growing at an appropriate pace. Most people who are able to carry on "usual daily activities" should do so. That's a kind of glue that keeps holding it all together.

We can't emphasize Service too much. *How do I serve?* is the question that should be uppermost in your mind, as your Awareness increases. It's all out in front of you. All you have to do is look for opportunities. And it isn't always helping those in obvious need. That's always an option and every opportunity should be taken. Baking good wholesome breads because you work at a bakery, or telling children that the world is a scary place right now and we're here to take care of each other. The list could go on, and on to include every positive, life-affirming activity you can think of. The bus drivers, the fundraisers, the repair people of all kinds. All interconnected, all a kind of glue holding the material world together.

C: Any other ways Awareness can be cultivated?

F: By connecting with other species. Learning about their pain — how they're suffering because of changing conditions. Many species will disappear in the coming wave of disruptive events, climate changes. That happens with each and every rebalance period in the planet's history. Once the population is diminished, once the dust settles, so to speak, on a whole new scenario of what is earth and what role our species has, if any, will require a broader perspective on what kind of world we want.

Some will survive and carry on. What that world will look like, I'm not privy to know. What I do know is that I'm alive here, watching all of this unfold in your world. It is good that you have opened yourself up to this greater reality. Let us help as many others as we can to do the same.

C: I will with my last breath.

F: That's what's being asked. You are doing it well, along with many others. Blessings on this great work.

Current Upheavals

F: We are fast entering the "chute" of acceleration — the birth canal, to use an analogy. Things will seem to happen faster, as they already appear to. Hard to keep up with all the news, the evolution of ideas, the "signs" of a greater understanding of multiple dimensions.

It will cause some to "pop," as you say. People who can't handle the pressure, the demand to expand or die. They choose to die and take others with them. Don't think [the people killed] are victims. They are martyrs just as surely as the people who gave their lives in wars to stop tyranny. Thank them. Honor them. This transition, like all others, has "casualties," but the others who wore uniforms and were part of deployments are easy to see as heroes. Individuals, people worshipping the All That Is in a mosque, a temple, not as easy to see as heroes, but they are.

The upheavals are getting closer to those yet unaffected. When it hits, it will be devastating to many.

C: What is "it?"

F: Calamities of all sorts. Food shortages, weather disruptions, whole industries impacted. There will be signs that the consensus reality of the world order is cracking up — becoming transparent — seen for what it is: a construction of the human mind that cannot abide the strains on the system's resources, weather patterns. Nothing that humans haven't endured before, only on a much bigger scale.

C: Please give us more guidelines on how to cope and be of service.

F: Begin with Awareness of what's going on. Depending on your location on the planet, you may know in excruciating detail what's happening — [if you're living in] Venezuela, Brazil, Yemen, North Korea. Or you have a vague awareness that the infrastructure is crumbling, as you say, but right now it's still holding up.

Letting in more and more of the Awareness of what is happening, if you have the luxury of doing so (our readers are obviously in that group), is something that must be done gradually. As you have been expanding your Awareness to include a greater reality, so too must others who hope to cope with the current upheavals. Taking it all in at once is not possible, nor desirable. Too much can cause a serious disruption in your life.

C: I've given up hope for any of the problems to be fixed. I subscribe to the hope that when the damage is done, has completed its destructive cycle, that it will be possible to begin again, to start over, with more consciousness, more compassion than the restart of other eras.

F: May it be so. There's no way for you or for me to know if that will come to pass. I believe that the more effort incarnates put into the collective consciousness bank account, so to speak, the more there will be to draw on when the revisioning and rebuilding begin.

These are lonesome times. Everyone is feeling cut off, isolated, alone in their concern for their loved ones, for their world. Many are aware on a psychic level that things are collapsing. It's a very scary time. There's no way around it. The part of the incarnate that is human, of the earth, feels the threat to survival and reacts accordingly.

Just be sure to include the windows of light along with the horror movies. It's all there, but it's easy to fall into the trap of screening for what you want to see — only the beautiful, or only the ugly. Earth is a masterpiece of paradox and an incarnate can do no better than be able to hold it all in a warm embrace and say, "Yes, this is our creation," with love.

Rebalance Is Always Part of a Cycle

C: What else can we give our readers?

F: We can tell them to lighten up. Yes, there are ominous clouds on the horizon. Yes, it's going to be a painful birthing process. But right this moment, if you can, think of something joyful, do something silly.

C: I love to buy helium balloons — butterflies, monkeys, birds — and have them floating in various rooms. They make me smile and lighten my day.

F: Precisely! And others will have their ways of bringing joy, beauty, music, that lights them up. Fill the space you live in with the Light and Love you want all to participate in. Your helium balloons send messages, invisible ones of course, but clear messages about how existence is about joy and God's Love that we all share.

Don't hesitate to bring Light into any situation.

C: What can you say to a person who is not feeling the threat of insecurity, or suffering from climate change, or getting a direct hit from the chaos swirling all over the planet? What can we say to such a person as preparation for things to come?

F: "*Namaste.* I see the divine within you, and you are fortunate to be able to focus on what probable reality you would like to bring into being." We are all co-creators of the realities we share, even the ugly, harmful ones. Your behavior, your thoughts, your constructions right now — of relationships and organizations — need to be illustrative of what kind of world you would like to project.

We know our audience, the ones who can afford books and choose to read them, are an elect slice of humanity. But that's all we can do in this overpopulated, over-stimulated world that so many beings have put together, for better or worse.

C: What can each of us who is aware and wants to react with the most appropriate response possible — what can we do?

F: Ask for help — from friends, from colleagues, certainly from family. Strengthen bonds of caring and openness to "what is true for you." Strengthen bonds of community support for those who will clearly be most challenged by the "crumbling infrastructure." The young, the elderly, the frail, those who are already battling a disease or condition that makes them less able to fend for themselves. Those kinds of responses from the more able are precisely the acts of compassion that will count toward the quality of your life. They will also model behavior for others who don't know what to do. Be like the man [prisoner] who passed out bread in the concentration camp* during WWII — he is remembered much more than those who simply gave up. Nothing wrong with giving up when the situation is impossible to improve. But even a few acts of kindness before the end will live on in the "akashic record." It is all recorded, you know — every act, every thought, although the records are of a much higher nature than your recording devices. [smile]

C: What new ideas can we create or bring into the situation that can help us get through the messiness of the challenges to come?

F: We can hold each other as divine. It's an old idea, going back thousands of years. But held by so few that it never had any widespread effect. We are each playing our role as a particle of God, of the creative force of the universe and beyond. We are co-creator in every sense. Participants in the great, and not so great, events of the lifetime we find ourselves in. We are Love; we are beings of Light. We are all connected in a grand Communion of Souls and beings beyond our imagination to hold each other as fellow particles, as [in] *I am the I AM.* That's a new idea. At least for 99.9% of humanity.

Deciding to Stay or Go

C: Do you have any idea what the "upheaval" period will demand of us?

F: It will take the best of the best to hold the consciousness of small groups into a loving, healing whole. Many will die as heroes trying to make that happen. It will contain a massive calling, a reckoning of sorts as to where each individual soul will show up. Humanity will be tested. Some will pass on to the greater reality knowing they held the line on the preservation of values as best they could. You will be one of them.

C: If someone who is in a very traumatic situation between survival and death, such as starving, how does that choice between fighting to survive and letting go, or committing suicide, get negotiated? Put another way, when you're in the push/pull of hard-wired survival and "going home," how do you decide?

F: You make it sound like a clear-cut choice. The line between them is blurry, fluid. Anything from the "outside" could come along and tip the scales, so to speak. Someone reaches out for help and you find the energy to respond. A dear one on the other side appears as an escort to take you home. You don't know what your own consciousness will provide. It's certainly not a rational choice. Just know that whatever happens is "right" in the moment. The physical space/time world is so filled with "shoulds" and ethics and moral codes that will get in the way of allowing the soul its choices, its best next step on its journey. Don't spend time planning ahead for your demise. You will get there and know what to do. I promise.

Pass the loaves and fishes now. People are spiritually malnourished. So many are not aware that we are all One, all carry a connection to the Divine within us, no matter what our behavior has been — saintly or criminal — people full of compassion as well as those full of hatred. That's hard to see when you're the victim of the hatred, but people do. Sometimes, not often, but sometimes a family can forgive someone who has murdered one of their family members. It's humbling to behold. That kind of forgiveness, that kind of Love that excludes no one, is available to each being.

[pause]

F: Tonight I also want to address the loneliness of people who are more frightened than they need to be about what's coming. People like you who have chosen to sustain the gaze, not only at climate change, but other aspects of the destruction/rebirth process on the horizon of planet Earth. [There's] so much to worry about, if you list them in a rational way. Best to hold the physical space/time dimension as a Whole. Those who feel isolated in their concerns, so difficult to tell others about this, so helpless to know what to do, if anything. I want to address some thoughts to them tonight.

C: Certainly.

F: I want to say, "You are not alone." If you could only see what I see in terms of links between individuals who don't know each other, groups who don't know others like them exist. It will all become clear as the pressure mounts to pitch in or check out. There will be many doing one or the other. The Go-Fund-Me responses are a clue. One little boy gets thrown off a balcony at a shopping mall — a cruel and insane act of one miserable individual — and thousands of people respond with love and financial support. That sentiment, that desire to demonstrate caring, love, solidarity — whatever you call it — exists deeply within the human soul.

※

On April 12, 2019, a five-year old boy was thrown off the third-floor balcony at the Great Mall of America in Bloomington, Minnesota. Landen fell 40 feet and landed on the floor below, sustaining multiple life-threatening injuries. The 24-year old perpetrator said at his arraignment that he came to the mall to do just that — looking to kill someone. Landen's family immediately put out a call for prayers over local TV and radio. A family friend started a GoFundMe site and money came pouring in to cover hospital expenses.

I [Cynthia] contributed, and received regular updates. Landen finally came out of critical care in early August. One month later he returned to his family home, still needing much rehab. The family called it "a miracle." Meanwhile, over 29,000 people had contributed, usually in small amounts, and the funding went over one million dollars. Landen went to kindergarten in November. He tells people all the time when they get hurt,

"Don't worry, I fell off a cliff, but Angels caught me and Jesus loves me, so I'm ok and you will be too!"

⁓◎⁓

C: There are thousands of hurting people all around us — homeless, living in RVs because of fires and floods, and suffering from acts of random violence.* There doesn't seem to be an outpouring commensurate with the cries for help.

F: You're right. There isn't. And there won't be enough people to respond adequately when upheavals are everywhere. People will be at their best. Some will be at their worst. That's the way it's always been in times of war and famine and plague. One comforting piece of wisdom may be to know all this has happened before. Massive species extinction — a cleansing, if you will — of life forms who have played out their DNA potential. Humans may be one of them.

The individuals who may survive will be of both kinds — the ones who are reservoirs of the collective wisdom deposited over millennia, and ones who will survive due to brute force and willpower.

You won't be in either category. You [Cynthia] will have sacrificed yourself and moved on because you have the knowledge of death as transition. Many others will have it too. Hopefully, we can help others to gain it through these books and make it easier. Everyone will make that transition one way or another. But it can be made with much less fear and with more anticipation of what's to come.

C: Thank you. Knowing that helps to keep me going.

F: I know. The pressure to give up is always present. The will and determination to keep on going until your time is up seems in short supply. It is not. Look at the young people, rising up to meet the climate challenge. But the opioid crisis is the shadow side of the dynamic — drug your pain until it's over. The choice is clear.

There is Life after Life. Most won't get that until they die to this world. The few who know beforehand will be those shining lights that lead the way. I don't mean to minimize suffering. There will be suffering. Suffering is nothing new to the earth plane. It's part of the curriculum. There have been horrible slaughters, plagues and events of Nature — earthquakes, volcanoes, at least one meteor [impact] that we know of that caused an enormous amount of damage and wiped out a huge percentage of the living species.

Yet we are here again — overpopulating, expanding ourselves into other species' habitat, using up the earth's resources like fools with no sense. It's all happened before, and it's going to happen again.

C: Knowing that death is a transition to an easier existence, at least while we're between incarnations, will be so comforting.

F: I'm here, in such an in-between place, and I can attest to its beauty, its grand-beyond-description temples of joy and sound and colors. God is here. God is everywhere — where you are too, because God is the All That is. The genius of the God who has created all of this — your reality and mine — is so astounding, and when we each realize that we are Gods — co-creators of what we experience — we will be able to handle any difficulties that come our way. You will too, and many of those who read our books will get the message and be grateful — certainly to us, but much more importantly, to the truth of what we're saying, and encourage people to find on their own. We provide blessings for their journeys.

Knowledge of the greater reality has been around for millennia, but only to a very small number of people who could look up from their survival work to step into the stars. Some have done that many times and are here now to be the harbingers of Light. But as I said at the end of *Book One*, we must light the lamp again because we're in a darkening period. So many martyrs have died. People who "took a bullet" literally to try to wake the rest of us up to the seething hatreds and greed that's taking over in so many places.

We are trying to warn incarnates too in our way — it's coming — the upheavals which will reshape the inhabitable areas of the planet for humans. Many more species of plants and animals will end their cycle. Remember: NOTHING IS LOST. The physical is discarded, composted, but even those atoms/molecules are preserved. We are inviolate beings, but we must not confuse our egos, our bodies, our personalities with the essence of our being. If you put on a blue coat, are you always identified as the blue-coat wearer? No, of course not. Changing our clothing is something we do easily. So too with personalities and preferences from lifetime to lifetime. Your body is a blue coat. Not an essential part of who you are.

EXERCISE: (STEP 6)

Setting up the contact scenario: Since this is an exercise in automatic writing, you are now ready to set what you need in place. Set the lighting in the room to be just barely bright enough to see what you write. If it's daylight, try to dim the light coming into the room. You will need to be sitting at a table at which you can write. Many have found it useful to have an object that is sacred to them. It can be anything from a rock to a religious symbol. If you are asking to contact a loved one on the other side, have a photograph of that person. Ideally, something that belonged to that person as well. If you are hoping to contact someone who you didn't know while that person was alive, such as an author or saint, have a book or picture symbolizing that person if possible.

The basic equipment is a tablet of paper and a pen. If you prefer you can have a laptop computer. A lit candle is a universal beacon for all who are calling on the greater reality. After you've gone through the steps in Exercises 1 through 5, hold the intention of contacting the other side. Ask yourself: "Will I allow my intuition to work? Do I believe I can do this automatic writing and get results?" If you get any "No" answers, just keep practicing the exercises (1-6) until all the answers are "Yes." Then you will be able to move on to make contact in Exercise 7.

What is time-bound? What is eternal?

⁓

If you get there before I do
Comin' for to carry me home
Tell all my friends I'm a-comin' too
Comin' for to carry me home.

— "Swing Low, Sweet Chariot"
(a Negro spiritual still sung in many churches today)

The question of what is impermanent and what is eternal has been explored since humans first looked up at a starry night sky. Those stars looked like they stay affixed to the firmament forever. However, it was plain to see that humans and other breathing beasts and all the plants around did not last forever. (We know now that stars don't last forever either. They just last longer.)

The main principle of *Book Two* has been that Consciousness is primary: the material level and space/time are expressions of a greater reality. We have implied that Consciousness is eternal. That's as much as we know now.

Maybe it's like the stars in the night sky — it just lasts longer. We can see in many ways that physical expressions within our realities are time-bound, temporary, impermanent. For incarnates, there is a huge gray area concerning what is our essential self and what is transitory. Many channeled materials — including Matthew McKay's automatic writing exchanges with his son Jordan in the book *Seeking Jordan** — speak of how certain personality characteristics stay with you "on the other side." Others such as grief, melancholy, despair fall away. Closely held biases such as racism, sexism, ageism, homophobia and xenophobia, or religious orthodoxies and stereotypes of all kinds may be slower to disappear. We hear of souls having to go to "rehab" to repair and heal those misguided separations of self from "other."

Frances tells us there are ways, while incarnate, to work on those denials of the One. How much better would it be to not drag those antipathies like old baggage into another lifetime?

C: What can we say about what is time-bound?

F: In the world of time we are struck by its passing parade. Things change slowly, or quickly. There is little certainty, especially these days, that tomorrow will be like today. That those things we count on — people, home, security, structures of all kinds — will hold. As we've been saying, they are wobbling. What we know is that all is change, all is impermanent, even the stars above.

While we are incarnate, we sense the passage of time marked by joys and pains. We see it in the changing faces of our loved ones and the growing of our friends' children from babies to middle-aged adults. What does not change is the eternal presence of God, of All That Is, and that particle we each represent and co-create.

C: How do we recognize the changing from the unchanging?

F: Love is abiding, expanding within us. Hatred comes and goes. Despair comes and goes. In most cases, grief comes and goes. There is nothing wrong with feeling those emotional states. They are "baked into" the duality of this particular planet. But there are qualities and experiences that feel so much more alive such as beauty, gratitude, joy and of course Love, that have an undergirding or foundational feel. Not for everyone, I know. There are people today who are suffering mightily, seeing family members being blown up, or starving to death.

You must understand that it's all part of the agreement to incarnate. It's a rough way to learn the lessons of the miraculous experiences — by contrast. But trust me, this is one form of "boot camp" in understanding our greater existence in an eternal reality.

C: What can you say about the eternal?

F: Before I go there, let me finish the temporal. When one's reality seems to pass by, to change like a kaleidoscope of images and moods, it's a way to grasp the essential nature of our participation in creation. Who is turning the scope? Who's changing the colors? Who's trying to fool us into thinking or acting in ways that are counterproductive to our evolution in Consciousness? Is it God? Some outside force? No. It's the beholder, the one who's *also* twisting the kaleidoscope mechanism. We are producing our own show, our own play, our own world. That's of course in concert with all the others we interact with. We are not individual creators, we are *co*-creators. When you realize that it's *you* changing the images and the moods, you may start to adjust it more carefully, more in line with your purpose, more in line with God's purpose — God being All There Is.

The passing of time, and the illusion of confined space, are a curriculum — one specifically designed for this particular lesson. If and when you "get it," then you graduate to a higher level, understanding that the time-bound is a lesson in the eternal, in a dualistic* format.

C: Thank you! So please say more about the eternal.

F: "Eternal" is a tricky word. So crude in what it's trying to capture, and here we are again without the vocabulary. It's not *forever* — that's just a time-bound word pretending to be a balance to "changing." But forever implies time passing.

Eternal is not some static state where nothing changes. That also is a mischaracterization.

So what can we say? The eternal is dynamic, but not linear. All is happening at once — even the past, present and future of the time-bound places. It doesn't *become*, it *is*. All at once and everywhere. (There we are using space/time words again.) Be that as it may, it's closer to a sense of focus and where you put your attention. If you put your focus on the "bad" parts of your current reality, you miss the beautiful. You are participating in a co-created reality, so you cannot avoid those [bad] parts. You can only work to shift it [toward beautiful] for yourself and others you want to join you. Maybe the best you can do in a dreadful environment is to hold each other and remind everyone you will be together again in another existence. That's an extreme but it is certainly happening [in some parts of your world].

A cancer ward, a homeless encampment, a war zone, to name a few very dire places, are co-created as well. Finding yourself in one of those is part of your journey. That may seem unkind to say, but it's true if it's your reality, and it's a horror you've chosen to endure because its rewards [for learning] are great. Hard as that may seem to grasp, it has direct experience in it. That does not at all excuse the moral lapses that may have co-created the scenario. Greed and hatred abound in setting up zones of suffering for many. But it cannot be stressed enough that this is all a co-created reality. It also teaches enormous amounts of Compassion to those not directly involved. We've pointed out a number of situations in this book that were awful, and in their creation of pain pours out Compassion and hopefully Wisdom to create a better reality.

The time-bound is a teacher. The eternal is a sorting out of the work of co-creating a harmonious Whole. We are all working on it. That is, those of us who still have a separate consciousness and who have not yet merged in the Oneness.

A New Frontier

C: How can we begin to "hold the tension of opposites" — the time-bound and the eternal?

F: Let's begin with a sense of the frontier we're facing. A frontier is an unexplored, unmapped place, at least for those approaching it. The greater reality is the frontier unexplored by most incarnates. You must be willing to take risks In this case, the risks may be a loss of comfort zone, of beliefs, about "the way things work," about what you hold as moral values, about how you hold the behaviors of others. Many more, but that's plenty for now.

C: Please say more about "exploring a new frontier."

F: Basically, you walk around the world you're familiar with and see it with new eyes — without labels or judgments, and ready to be surprised. Traditional risk-taking requires courage and some measure of self-control and confidence in one's own integrity. All that is necessary here too, in the greater reality. But with "new eyes" you sense the difference between your normal consensus reality and [encountering] unexpected situations.

C: Such as?

F: Such as [having] a conversation with someone not incarnate anymore, who can talk with you as if they were physically present. You have to be ready to suspend your disbelief, your fear of "dead people," most of all your own limitations in defining what's real and what's not. It's a *greater* reality.

C: What are the advantages of that kind of exploration, that foray into a new frontier?

F: Meeting God. Not some old person in long robes. But the omnipresent infusion of Love into every molecule and energy frequency you can fathom. Imagine a fish in water. We suppose the fish has no consciousness of being in water, the same way human incarnates have little or no awareness of being in air, unless there's a shortage of it.

Being in God's presence, or in the All That Is, or in the Oneness of All Being — by whatever name — it's the first and most powerful experience you can have when you break the bonds of space/time physical reality. It's a matter of degree as well. Your first conscious experience, as with people who have near-death experiences and can report back, is an excitement and a wonder that such an experience can and does exist.

Saints take lifetimes to perfect the comings and goings of that experience, without the need for an NDE. But we are here to dispel that notion that it takes lifetimes of arduous practice to taste the divine. You as a human carry that divine spark within you every moment, and it's there to access. In the coming days, most of earth's inhabitants will have access to that part of themselves or else fall prey to all manner of fears and survival behaviors. Your world is having crises on a daily basis — hurricanes, fires, floods, violence with mass killings — and what most often happens? Suffering, to be sure. But also Love, Community, and "How can I help?" Outpouring of money and volunteers of all kinds. Kindness, heroic actions that sometimes result in death of the hero.

The chaos engenders panic and fear, but also opens the doors of Love and Light pouring in that wouldn't be possible without the conditions of need showing up.

C: We can't minimize the pain, the losses.

F: Nor can we minimize the opportunities that arise to serve at levels unavailable in ordinary times.

C: Is that why the Current Upheavals are happening?

F: It's part of the reason. But a more important factor is the necessity of balance — of regaining a sense of what it means to live in harmony with each other and with the Earth that doesn't have the aspect of exploitation involved. Right now the situation is so far from that. Everyone knows it on some level, and accepts, if not willingly, that it cannot go on.

C: What can help us endure this "rebalance?"

F: The theme of Aliveness would be useful to those who come to know and live their sense of inviolate soul in a context of eternity –- infinite creativity to make new worlds and become a citizen in a much larger field of being.

It's so important to hold the life you have lightly as you approach the transition [to life after life]. I don't mean [that you should] give up on your life. But to see it as a final stage, at whatever age you die, for making your fullest contribution.

The upheavals are growing closer. So widespread. People "cracking up," committing suicide, those are the "small" signs. [Larger signs such as] mass starvations and countries falling into authoritarian measures to try to hold together. It will take many forms. Let me repeat what I've said before — keep doing what's in front of you as best you can, with the highest consciousness you can muster. You are inputting that wisdom and compassion, and acts of service into the collective Whole. That's God in action. There is no separate GOD, just all of us, on many levels we can't fathom who are working in concert to make this Earth transition as fruitful as it can be. Earth needs a rest too, from all the physical harm She has experienced. She needs to heal Herself and She will. We can all help. We must be willing to do whatever we can, including die for Her, as so many have already. It is a rebalance.

Being Prepared

F: Each person will soon have to reckon with themselves on how they will respond when the time comes to face the destruction of their world (the one they have constructed around them).

We must do our best to encourage those who will survive to take the best of themselves and human evolution — wisdom, morality, beauty, and so on — into the new world, in whatever form it takes for them. Those who drown in fears will not survive anyway, whatever debris they cling to (authoritarian leaders, silos in Kansas,* isolated areas that cannot feed themselves). They will perish as this phase of Earth's evolution goes into its winter, shudders and dies a proper death and resurrects in the Spring as it has done, and will continue to do.

C: What stands out for me is: be prepared to die.

F: It's not that stark. It's preparation on a psychological level, as when one enters the military or becomes a police officer or a fire fighter, or goes to volunteer where there's an epidemic going on. You may not die in that line of work, but the presence of that knowledge adds a dimension of courage and willingness to sacrifice yourself if necessary.

So many people have been in that self-sacrificing position. It's not new in human history. Not at all. It's just new to the current situation where things still look "normal."

When structures start to crumble, like all the glaciers melting on Earth these days, the pace picks up, and what seems solid a few weeks ago is suddenly exposed as fragile and about to give way. Just know that that's the situation you all are facing. What you count on as stability could suddenly seem as less so, or maybe not at all.

People will be helping people — all over the world. It will not turn into a chaotic, violent situation overnight. There will be pockets of violence, no doubt.

C: In a middle-of-the-night message, you spoke of me as a leader, or at least a voice in the orchestration of leaders around the world. Can you say more about the role I can play?

F: You're doing it now. Your job is to let those who can hear the message of death as transition take it in so that it can alleviate some of the fear and suffering that will be widespread. Make your voice heard in as many ways as possible. This will be an orchestration, a Greek chorus of voices,* playing the role of the balcony perspective.

Much will be left to the individuals whose lives will be upended. You'll hear of miracles being performed, as the Bible tells us Jesus did. Multiplying loaves and fishes to feed a crowd. Having appropriate apparitions showing up to provide guidance and the bigger picture of what's going on.

Also, Gaia will be more active with all this energy released. So much pent-up energy in people trying to hold the consensus reality together. When that starts to break down, to let go, earthquakes and volcanoes will become more active.

C: Sounds like an end-of-the-world scenario.

F: It is, and will be for many. But not the coming of the Messiah in the traditional sense — more of a rebalancing of the lopsided yang energies that have disrupted the flow of yin and yang. Too much yang. It results in hostilities and greed and hatred among people. That must end. It will. There will be a contingent who will carry the hard-fought-for values of social justice, and beauty, and love relationships into a new era. They may think they're still on planet Earth, but they could be somewhere else. The universe has many, many dimensions.

> *As I return home to that other earth;*
> *return earth to that other home —*
>
> — LISA SMARTT & MORTON FELIX,
> *Veil: Love Poems from Across the Threshold*

EXERCISE: (STEP 7)

Making initial contact: Know that you can accept or reject anything that comes through this process. Souls on the other side are in varying degrees of development, just as those on this side.

Move through the exercises (Steps 1-6).

Then begin with: "Are you there?" Have a few more questions ready for your first encounter. Be prepared to write down anything that enters the clear, empty space in your mind. If a stray thought enters such as "This is not going to work," take a few breaths, empty your mind again and wait patiently. It is important to remember that you will not *hear* words. Channeling is a form of telepathy between two beings. There will be words as thought forms but no sounds. Write down whatever you receive. It's natural to be a little scared by trying this new activity. You will be fine. Your spirit guides are with you and you are protected. It's a new adventure.

The experience may last a few minutes or much longer. After the session is finished, see what was communicated.

*Those of the spirit world are trying very hard to let us know that they're here. But so many of us don't sense them. **So what a blessing it is for those in the spirit world** when somebody goes to the effort of connecting with them and delivering their messages!*

— SUZANNE GIESEMANN, author, evidential medium, speaker, and former US Navy Commander

Epilogue

Death is not extinguishing the light;
it is putting out the lamp because dawn has come.

— Rabindranath Tagore, Bengali poet

Tagore's declaration refers to Life after Life, and captures the theme of *Seven Questions, Book One*. In that book's closing pages, Frances exhorts us:

> *"Now it is time to relight the lamp — your being — because darkness is setting in again, and there's work to be done in the recesses of our minds and hearts while a dark night passes."*

She saw, along with many others who have the courage to look, that a period of darkness was approaching. To paraphrase the theme of *Book Two*, you *are* Conscious Light. And the body you have is the container with which to hold the lamp.

Now, at the end of *Book Two*, we understand even more that the Light is sorely needed. In this book, we come to recognize that the "lamp" is us, radiating the Light within us. The Light shines forth compassion and wisdom — our divine co-creating nature. The word "Light" appears over fifty times in this volume, including Festivals of Light, "light-bulbness," the light at the end of the tunnel, beings of Light, and time to light the lamp again. Alongside the Lights, there are many references to current upheavals. As the production team was preparing this book for publication, the COVID-19 virus was enveloping the planet. It clearly is an "upheaval."

For some, bringing the Light means working in areas where chaos and suffering and violence prevail. For others, it means being at the front line of a service organization, at border crossings, and in nurseries where newborns are going through opioid withdrawal. Frances also suggests that for many, being the lamp means being the best version of ourselves that we can be, holding together a wobbly planet. Whatever form it may take, be the lamp whenever and wherever you can.

This book is not simply offering a way to navigate a difficult transition period where much will be uncertain. It's also an opportunity to clear out old beliefs, as well as to co-create new realities for lifetimes spent in harmony with ourselves, our fellow humans, and the Earth's community of other species.

Frances and I have already begun work on *Book Three* of the *Seven Questions* trilogy. She's already given me the theme: **You are not alone**. A few days after I got that message, I came across song lyrics from the 1945 musical *Carousel* written by Rodgers and Hammerstein: "You'll Never Walk Alone."* It inspires us to go forth in the storm with our heads held high. We will discover who our companions are on this journey.

Parting Thoughts

From Frances: The more people we can inform about the existence of *Seven Questions*, the more stability we will add to the current situation. There's nothing wrong with trying to stabilize the ship so that as many people as possible can reach the lifeboats and receive help. Knowing that there is Life After Life will help so many cope better now. It's similar to enduring a tough winter because you *can* count on Spring showing up at some point. What if winter went on and on, and you had no idea if and when Spring would come?

Despair. Depression. Suicide. One of the most beautiful things about living on Planet Earth is trusting that Spring does come. You can absolutely count on it.

That's why you [C] chose the name "Spring." It was a symbol of your purpose. You are a harbinger, along with many millions of others, of the Spring to come, whether that be on earth or in heaven. And by "heaven," I mean not just one limited place but the infinite expanse of dimensions to choose from. We are all inhabitants of a much larger "green space" than we can ever imagine. Earth contains tiny suggestions of what the greater reality offers. But only tiny glimpses. An enormous experience awaits each being, each soul, each particle of consciousness. Nothing is lost.

From Cynthia: I am Consciousness. I am participating in creating my own reality, and co-creating a reality with my fellow participants of all species. I am unique and yet I also share the dreams of my other co-creators. One of the lessons I'm here to learn in this incarnation is how to co-create a reality that works toward the evolution of each individual soul, including mine, while at the same time embracing the harmony and cohesion of the whole.

I am unique because no other being has the same elements of experience, lifetimes, lessons learned, lessons failed, and hopes and dreams for future incarnations. At this point in my life, I am a messenger of Light. May it be so.

～◎

There will be a *Seven Questions, Book Three*. Goodbye for now.

Glossary

Automatic writing is the ability to produce written words via telepathy without deliberate conscious thought. The person doing the writing receives whole thoughts from a source outside themselves — perhaps a deceased relative, spouse or friend — or even a complete stranger. To the receiver, it feels like taking dictation. The receiver writes it out in their own hand or types it on a keyboard.

Channeling is the practice of entering a meditative or trancelike state in order to receive messages from a spiritual guide or other discarnate being. The messages can be written, as in automatic writing, or simply spoken by the channeler. When a channeler assumes a voice, speech patterns, or the personality of the source, they are more often termed a "medium."

Cosmology is the study of how the physical universe came into existence and how it works.

Discarnate means a person or entity not presently (or ever) in a human body.

Dualism (also duality) is the belief that reality consists of two irreducible, irreconcilable elements or modes — a "duality." A familiar example would be the philosopher René Descartes' separation of mind and matter. In a religious context the universe may be believed to be under the dominion of two opposing principles: good and evil. More common examples might include right/wrong and subject/object.

Incarnate, as a noun, refers to a soul living in a body; as a verb, to incarnate means to take on a lifetime in a body.

Lifetimes refers to multiple lifetimes of the same entity. Viewed from within a linear space/time reality, they are perceived as individual, past, present, or future. Viewed from beyond space/time they are perceived as happening simultaneously.

Near-Death Experience (NDE) is a term coined by Dr. Raymond Moody, in his book *Life After Life* (1976). It refers to a person being conscious despite having been declared clinically dead, i.e., having no respiration, heartbeat, or detectable brainwave activity. A person who experiences an NDE later returns to physical life and describes a variety of experiences. These may include observation of their own physical body or the physical environment from an external vantage point. Many accounts contain some version of traveling to a nonphysical environment filled with light and love.

Often the experiencer reports not wanting to return to their body and/or being given a choice of returning, or not. But return they did, eager to describe their own view of heaven and the afterlife. Those who tell their NDE stories in books say that they have a deeper appreciation of life and a greatly diminished fear of death.

Nonlocal consciousness means awareness and volition not connected with, or dependent upon, a body or brain and therefore independent of space and time. In the realm of non-local consciousness, communication has no boundaries and is instantaneous. Aspects of quantum physics demonstrate a similar independence from normal space and time.

Out-of-Body Experience (OBE) is a term that was coined by parapsychology researcher Charles T. Tart in the early 1970s to describe reports from people who said they left their physical bodies and were able to see, hear, and move about in another kind of body, as well as in nonphysical dimensions of reality. Prior to this term, which came to be the most popular one, this phenomenon was called *astral travel* or *spiritual travel*. Tart worked with Robert Monroe, who described his OB experiences in three books, beginning in 1971. *(See References)*

Oversoul is defined in the transcendentalism of Ralph Waldo Emerson as a spiritual essence or vital force in the universe in which all souls participate and that therefore transcends individual consciousness. In the books by Jane Roberts channeling Seth, the word *oversoul* is used in a narrower sense of a grouping of souls who incarnate individually and share the learnings of that incarnation with the others upon return Home. This is also referred to as **Group Soul**.

Remote Viewing (RV) is the direct psychic perception of an aspect of the physical world without the use of normal physical senses. In people with well-developed RV talent, time and distance are not barriers to perception. Many parapsychology researchers have written about RV experiments, including Russell Targ, Stephan Schwartz, and Charles T. Tart.

> *"Being psychic is simply being more sensitive to the sea around us. It's simply a method that allows for an additional sense of being."*
>
> — Joe McMoneagle, army officer and remote viewer for the CIA during the 1980s. From his book *Mind Trek*, p. 113.

Shard: A shard is a fragment of a larger whole, i.e., a shard of broken glass. In some channeled works it refers to an individual member of a soul group, usually one that has taken on an incarnation.

Space/Time is a way of representing the four-dimensional reality that we inhabit. Putting the words together as a unit better illustrates the unity we usually experience.

Soul Group is a term used for an individual soul that expresses itself in a variety of ways, including an expression within three-dimensional reality. That physical expression is not by any means the entire soul. It is a fraction of the soul or a shard that participates as one source of information and creativity for the whole soul. In *Seven Questions*, we use "Soul Group" to indicate one soul with many subselves. **Group Soul** refers to a collection of souls who exist together and often share incarnate lifetimes together. In the channeling literature, these terms are sometimes used interchangeably.

Spirit guides are individual souls who were assigned, or have chosen, to provide guidance, assistance and protection to an incarnate being during his or her lifetime. They may also help in the transition from physical life to the afterlife.

Please be aware that these terms and definitions vary somewhat in the literature, and in any case are words on a page, not the reality that is beyond our comprehension

Endnotes

Aids in reading text: References to people or events in the text that are noted with an * can be found here in the Endnotes. Full details on sources are listed in the **Source References** section.

Cover: We are spiritual beings having a human experience. This subtitle comes from a quote often attributed to the French Jesuit philosopher, Pierre Teilhard de Chardin (1881-1955). However, the highly useful resource *quoteinvestigator.com* says there is no record of Teilhard writing that or saying those words, although it would certainly fit with his famous essay: *The Phenomenon of Man.* For more on Teilhard, see Wikipedia entry on his history. Other writers have claimed that quote.

Introduction

"In the alternative...." Willis Harman, *Higher Creativity: Liberating the Unconscious for Breakthrough Insights,* p. 187.

"Are we a body.... Just like a program...." Ervin Laszlo, *Intelligence of the Cosmos,* pp. 14-15.

"When someone's body...." Heaven and Hell by Emanuel Swedenborg (current edition), originally published in 1758. Paragraph #445.

"These bodies we live in...." Ram Dass, quote taken from website newsletter, 3-1-20, *www.ramdass.org* (Ram Dass made his transition on 12-22-19).

Opioid statistics at National Safety Council website: *www.nsc. org/opioids*

Question 1

(Opening quote) *"You are creatures of light...,"* One, a novel, by Richard Bach, p. 150.

Near-death experience (See **Glossary**)

Jane Roberts was an American author and poet who channeled, from 1963 to 1984, an entity who called himself Seth. Together they produced over a dozen books that covered the nature of reality, death, other dimensions, and how to hold events on earth in a larger frame. Many New Age authors, including Marianne Williamson and Deepak Chopra, credit the books with being a constant source of knowledge and inspiration.

Reference to *The Four Horsemen*. This image is found in both the Old and New Testaments of the Judeo-Christian Bible. In the Book of Ezekiel, the four horsemen stand for death by war, famine, pestilence and violence.

Exercise Step 1. The complete set of seven exercises for automatic writing appears on p. 159.

Question 2

(Opening quote) *"The reason why death...."* From Raymond Moody, p. 96.

"When I go to my death...." From *waiting to die*, by Kenneth Ring, p. 42.

The Life Review section can be found in *Book One* on p. 72.

Biblical citation: Solomon story, 1 Kings 3: 16-28.

Question 3

(Opening quote) *"When you enter time...."* From *The Individual and the Nature of Mass Events,* Jane Roberts/Seth, p. 127 (top paragraph), p. 215 (bottom paragraph).

New Testament story of loaves and fishes, Mark 8:16-21.

Edison's failed lightbulbs.... Edison himself said he tried "almost 1000" variations before he found the one that worked. See *https://en.wikipedia.org/wiki/Thomas_Edison*

News story of man and daughter drowned in Rio Grande River can be found at:
https://www.washingtonpost.com/world/2019/06/26/father-daughter-who-drowned-border-dove-into-river-desperation/

Om mani padme hum is a Sanskrit mantra. The first word, *Aum/Om,* is a sacred syllable in various *Indian religions.* The word *Mani* means "jewel" or "bead," *Padme* is the "*lotus flower*" (the Buddhist sacred flower), and *Hum* represents the *spirit* of *enlightenment.* The mantra's meaning shifts, depending on which branch of Buddhism is using it. Generally, it is an invocation to the Goddess of Compassion, Avalokiteshvara. For more information, look up the mantra in Wikipedia.org.

Question 4

(Opening quote) "*Listen closely for the departed....*" From *Veil: Love Poems from Across the Threshold,* by Lisa Smartt and Morton Felix, p. 79.

"*Some years ago....*" Story used with permission from Justine Willis Toms.

"*Greek chorus*": Frances makes a reference several times to a chorus of voices who function as the chorus did in ancient Greek plays. The chorus stood either to the side, or on a balcony above the stage, and offered background or summary information to help the audience follow the performance. Frances suggests that the hundreds of channelers around the world function as that kind of chorus.

Reference to Bob Monroe: Robert Monroe was the author of three books on journeys out-of-body, as well as Founder of The Monroe Institute in Charlottesville, VA.

"*you are right when you feel me there....*" From *Veil,* p. 53.

"*The vast majority....*" Jon Klimo, *Channeling: Investigations on Receiving Information from Paranormal Sources,* p. 211.

Rumi quote is reprinted in hundreds of places. Original source is unknown.

Question 5

(Opening) Christopher Fry, segment from his play, *A Sleep of Prisoners*. Taken from the website *www.gratefulness.org* (Brother David Steindl-Rast).

"When you enter time...." Jane Roberts/Seth, *The Individual and the Nature of Mass Events*, p. 127.

"Love is all you need...." If you're of a certain age, you may have heard the melody from the Beatles' song as you read these words. The song lyric transcends popular music and harkens to the eternal.

"Our deepest fear...." Marianne Williamson quote taken from her book: *A Return to Love: Reflections on the Principles of "A Course in Miracles."* NY: HarperCollins, 1996.

Virginia Satir quote was published as a poster by Celestial Arts in 1973. See *https://satirglobal.org/product/goals-for-me/*

Question 6

(Opening quote) *"The purpose of life...."* From Maria Montessori, Italian educator, whose vision for a different approach to the education of younger children resulted in Montessori schools being established all over the world. For more details on her pedagogy, see: *https://en.wikipedia.org/wiki/Maria_Montessori*

In 1990, J. K. Rowling was on a crowded train from Manchester to London when the idea for Harry suddenly "fell into her head." Rowling gives an account of the experience on her website:

> *I had been writing almost continuously since the age of six but I had never been so excited about an idea before. I simply sat and thought, for four (delayed train) hours, and all the details bubbled up in my brain, and this scrawny, black-haired, bespectacled*

boy who did not know he was a wizard became more and more real to me.

See: *www.jkrowling.com* and *www.Wikipedia.com* under Harry Potter

People "pop" from too much stress in their lives every day. The US has the most gun violence per capita of any country in the world. As an example, every year, the Center for Disease Control and Prevention releases the official number of people who were killed by guns in the United States. In 2018, that number was **39,741 people who died from gun violence. To put that in perspective, 40,000** people can fill **97** Boeing 747 jets; **40,000** students would fill **556** school buses.

The story of the man in the concentration camp is told by Viktor Frankl in his book *Man's Search for Meaning* (New York: Washington Square Press, 1988).

"One little boy gets thrown off a balcony at a shopping mall"— The story of Landen: *https://www.cbsnews.com/news/mall-of-america-balcony-boy-landen-continuing-to-fight-donations-gofundme/*

Also the ongoing GoFundMe story can be found at *https://gofundme.com* (search for Fundraiser for Landens [sic] family).

Question 7

"If you get there before I do...." This verse comes from what is perhaps the best-known Negro spiritual, *Swing Low, Sweet Chariot.* It's still sung in many churches today. Gospel music was built on the hope of reuniting decimated families and communities in heaven. *Swing Low, Sweet Chariot* lyrics: see *www.negrospirituals. com.* The origin of the song is ambiguous, but it's believed to have been written by a Choctaw freedman in Oklahoma, around 1862.

See more on *Seeking Jordan* by Matthew McKay in **References**.

Reference to silos in Kansas is the story of an old set of silos that housed nuclear missiles and has been turned into a shelter against nuclear attack and natural disasters. Residents can grow their own food and relax in luxury. *https://archinect.com/news/article/150095758/developer-brings-luxury-condos-to-old-missile-silos-in-kansas*

as I return home.... from *Veil: Love Poems from Across the Threshold,* by Lisa Smartt and Morton Felix, p. 47.

"Those of the spirit world...." From Suzanne Giesemann, author, evidential medium, speaker, and former Navy Commander. Quote taken from her website: *https://suzannegiesemann.com*

Epilogue

"You'll Never Walk Alone," the song from the 1945 musical *Carousel*, written by Richard Rodgers and Oscar Hammerstein II, has been recorded by over 100 artists as diverse as Frank Sinatra, Johnny Cash, Aretha Franklin, and opera star Renee Fleming, who sang it at Barack Obama's inauguration in January, 2009.

Reference to Greek choir again. See Endnote under Question 4.

Seven Steps to Automatic Writing

With the Tongues of Men and Angels: A Study of Channeling, by Arthur Hastings. NY: Holt, Reinhart and Winston, 1991. p. 203.

Source References

Seven Questions about Life After Life, Book One, by Cynthia Spring and Frances Vaughan. Wisdom Circles Publishing, 2019.

Channeling: Investigations on Receiving Information from Paranormal Sources, by Jon Klimo, 2nd edition. Berkeley, CA: North Atlantic Books, 1998.

Children Who Remember Previous Lives: A Question of Reincarnation, by Ian Stevenson. Revised edition. Jefferson, NC: McFarland & Co., 2000.

Heaven and Hell, by Emanuel Swedenborg. Originally published in 1758. Translated by John C. Ager (published in 1900), Pantianos Classics.

Higher Creativity: Liberating the Unconscious for Breakthrough Insights, by Willis Harman and Howard Rheingold. Los Angeles: Jeremy Tarcher, 1984.

The Individual and the Nature of Mass Events, by Jane Roberts/Seth. Reissue edition. San Rafael, CA: Amber-Allen Publishing, 1995.

The Intelligence of the Cosmos: Why Are We Here? New Answers from the Frontiers of Science, by Ervin Laszlo. Rochester, VT: Inner Traditions/Bear & Company, 2017.

Life After Life, by Raymond Moody, Jr., M.D. New York: Bantam Books, 1975.

One, a novel, by Richard Bach. New York: Dell Publishing, 1988.

Opening to Channel: How to Connect with Your Guide, by Sanaya Roman and David Packer. Novato, CA: H. J. Kramer, 1987.

Seeking Jordan: How I Learned about Death and the Invisible Universe, by Matthew McKay. Novato, CA: New World Library, 2016.

Veil: Love Poems from Across the Threshold, by Lisa Smartt and Morton Felix, University of Heaven, 2018.

waiting to die: A Near-Death Researcher's (Mostly Humorous) Reflections on His Own Endgame, by Kenneth Ring. Tucson, Arizona: Wheatmark, 2019.

With the Tongues of Men and Angels: A Study of Channeling, by Arthur Hastings. NY: Holt, Reinhart and Winston, 1991.

Additional References

A Course in Miracles: Text, Workbook and Manual for Teachers, channeled by Helen Schucman. Mill Valley, CA: first published by the Foundation for Inner Peace, 1975.

The Four-Fold Way, by Angeles Arrien. NY: HarperCollins, 1993.

The Nature of Personal Reality, by Jane Roberts/Seth. San Rafael, CA: Amber-Allen, reprinted 1994.

The Sufi Book of Life: 99 Pathways of the Heart for the Modern Dervish, by Neil Douglas-Klotz. New York: Penguin, 2005.

- **Books by Robert Monroe**

  Journeys Out of the Body. New York: Doubleday, 1971.

  Far Journeys. New York: Doubleday, 1985.

  Ultimate Journey. New York: Doubleday, 1994.

- **Books by John Mack**

  Abduction: Human Encounters with Aliens. NY: Scribner, 1994.

  Passport to the Cosmos: Human Transformation and Alien Encounters. NY: Three Rivers Press, 2000.

- **Books and Films Related to After-Death Communication (ADC)**

  Books:

  The Afterlife Interviews, Volumes I and II, by Jeffrey Marks. North Bend, OR: Arago Press, 2012 and 2014. Medium and researcher Marks created a set of 52 questions and then asked the questions of 14 spirits related to his incarnate clients. Although the discarnates had been from a variety of backgrounds, Marks was able to find common themes in the answers.

The Afterlife Revolution, by Whitley and Anne Strieber. Walker & Collier, Inc. 2017. These two people, married for 45 years, promised each other that the first one to die would contact the still-incarnate one with a series of clues, and then ongoing dialogues, and they did. This book is highly readable and Anne does a fine job of describing "the other side," much like Frances does in this book.

An End to Upside Down Thinking: Dispelling the Myth That the Brain Produces Consciousness, and the Implications for Everyday Life, by Mark Gober. Waterside Press, 2018. Gober came from the world of investment banking to explore the notion that consciousness creates all material reality. He explores a diverse set of disciplines, from psychic phenomena to quantum physics. A brief section on ADC. Received very high praise from best-selling authors of books in this area of exploration.

Hello from Heaven: A new field of research — After-Death Communication — confirms that life and love are eternal, by Bill Guggenheim and Judy Guggenheim. New York: Bantam Books, 1995. These two researchers collected more than 3300 personal accounts from people who firmly believed that they'd been contacted by loved ones who had died. This book contains 353 of the most powerful accounts.

The Immortal Mind: Science and the Continuity of Consciousness beyond the Brain, by Ervin Laszlo. Rochester, VT: Inner Traditions, 2014. This book came out prior to Laszlo's *The Intelligence of the Cosmos,* which Frances and Cynthia use as a source book for this one. *The Immortal Mind* lays the groundwork for the exploration of how consciousness can exist without connection to a living organism.

The Light Between Us: Stories from Heaven, Lessons for the Living, by Laura Lynne Jackson. NY: Spiegel & Grau, 2016. This is a lovely, accessible book by a woman who's a high school English teacher and a psychic medium. She helps people by conversing with their departed loved ones and exploring our connections with the other side.

One Mind: How Our Individual Mind Is Part of a Greater Consciousness and Why It Matters, by Larry Dossey, M.D. Carlsbad, CA: Hayhouse, 2016. This book explores a wide variety of phenomena: from near-death experiences, to dowsing, to psychic healing and whether ghosts exist. Dossey is best known for his controlled studies of the power of prayer to help heal someone who is ill. (It does!)

Words at the Threshold: What We Say as We're Nearing Death, by Lisa Smartt (Novato, CA: New World Library, 2017). Most of Lisa's book is about what people say just before they die. She has a fine chapter on ADC, including stories of people receiving messages, or having odd occurrences and "synchronicities," right after a loved one has passed.

Films:

Calling Earth. This remarkable 95-minute feature documentary introduces us to communication with the other side via electronic devices (recorders, telephones, TVs, computers, etc.). This phenomenon, known as Instrumental Trans-Communication (ITC), has been well documented at least since the 1950s and provides robust objective evidence for an afterlife. *Calling Earth* was produced by award-winning filmmaker Daniel Drasin. You can see it for free at *vimeo. com/101171248*. A five-minute preview is available at *tinyurl. com/callearth-preview*

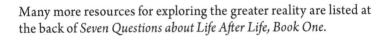

Many more resources for exploring the greater reality are listed at the back of *Seven Questions about Life After Life, Book One.*

Seven Steps to Automatic Writing

This automatic writing exercise, separated into seven steps, is a synthesis of material from several sources:

- How-to instructions given at a lecture by Matthew McKay, author of *Seeking Jordan*.
- *Channeling,* by Jon Klimo.
- Instructions for achieving higher consciousness given by The Monroe Institute in their *Gateway* program.
- *Opening to Channel,* by Sanaya Roman and Duane Packer.

Step 1

Sit in a quiet, comfortable place where you won't be disturbed. If you have a practice of meditation, begin that process of clearing your mind. If you're not accustomed to doing this, it will take a few minutes longer. Let go of all other concerns and thoughts. Watch yourself breathe in and out slowly, with your abdomen rising and falling. Make sure your body is completely relaxed. Check for tension first in your lower body, then in your upper body. Then imagine that you occupy more space than simply your physical body. Your consciousness extends beyond your body.

If you feel yourself getting nervous, stop at this point.

Repeat the opening part of the exercise (clearing your mind, watching your breath, imagining your consciousness extending beyond your body) until you are centered and ready to **name** the contact you would like to make. This could be your higher self, a spirit guide, or someone who was incarnate and has passed on. Keep holding that open field, and let your choice of contact show up. Do not try to "think it." Let it appear. Hold the intention of contacting your desired connection. Ask yourself why you are seeking this experience. Repeat this exercise in upcoming days until you feel completely comfortable with your sense of an expanded self, and your choice of contact.

If it happens that you start receiving a telepathic message that seems to be coming from another source, then you are on your way. Go to *Good Questions to Ask* on p. 68 to find suggestions for opening the conversation. Most people who begin this process do not receive an immediate response. But don't rule it out.

Step 2

Raising your vibrational level: Your intention is to make contact at the highest possible level of your soul's development. You are focused entirely on an inner space. Locate that spark of divinity that resides in each and every soul. Let that spark expand until it turns into a strong sense of Light emanating from you. Fill yourself with the presence of Love that permeates the universe. Deeply sense that this exercise in making connection with nonphysical spirits has happened easily for millions of people throughout time. It is about opening, not efforting.

Focus on your intention to contact someone through automatic writing. You will succeed if you ask respectfully and your intention is to benefit your highest self and also be in service to All That Is.

Step 3

Setting up the channel of communication: In this exercise, you will need to ground yourself as well as create an image of a golden antenna reaching into the universe.

There are many ways to ground yourself. Find the one that works best for you. You can imagine you have roots growing down from your feet into the earth, firmly anchored. Another image is of long threads of golden energy originating in your pelvic area and reaching down into the earth, where they meet in a golden ball. If you have a mantra you say regularly, such as *Om mani padme hum*, repeating that can be used to ground you. A certain selection of music may work well, or perhaps a recording of environmental sounds such as easy waves on a seashore.

Now you are ready to set up the golden antenna or tube of light that will connect you with your contact. From the top of your head, imagine a golden beam shooting straight up into the sky and beyond. If someone were to be looking from the moon they would see that golden light coming from you and disappearing into the cosmos. Practice this exercise until the image comes easily and you can hold it steadily. Then imagine yourself as a radio receiver, picking up intelligent signals. Finish this sentence: "I am asking for this connection to [*name*] in order to [*fill in purpose*]."

For example, "I, Cynthia, am asking for this connection to Frances so that I may better understand the greater reality beyond the space/time dimension."

Step 4

Protection for crossing into the channeling process: Know that higher-level guides and contacts have your well-being as their main concern. At this step in the process, you'll make sure that you are connecting to the entity you've asked for, or a being who will be a source of guidance and clarity for your highest self.

After you have practiced Steps 1, 2, and 3, you are ready to "knock on the door." But first ask your own spirit guides for protection from any negative energies. Here is part of the affirmation used by students at the Monroe Institute when they are working on out-of-body exercises:

I deeply desire the assistance of those individuals whose wisdom, development, and experience are equal to or greater than my own. I ask their guidance and protection from any influence or any source that might provide me with less than my stated desires.

It will be useful to memorize the protection request so you can say it as needed, and confidently.

Step 5
Setting your intention: Finish this sentence: "I am asking for this connection to [name] in order to [ ]."

For example, "I, Cynthia, am asking for this connection to Frances so that I may better understand the greater reality beyond the space/time dimension."

At this step in the process, we're making sure that you will be connected to the entity you've asked for, or a being who will be a source of guidance and clarity for your highest self. Practice Steps 1 through 5 until you are very comfortable with the process.

Step 6
Setting up the contact scenario: Since this is an exercise in automatic writing, you are now ready to set what you need in place. Set the lighting in the room to be just barely bright enough to see what you write. If it's daylight, try to dim the

light coming into the room. You will need to be sitting at a table at which you can write. Many have found it useful to have an object that is sacred to them. It can be anything from a rock to a religious symbol. If you are asking to contact a loved one on the other side, have a photograph of that person — ideally, something that belonged to that person as well. If you are hoping to contact someone whom you didn't know while that person was alive, such as an author or saint, have a book or picture symbolizing that person if possible.

The basic equipment is a tablet of paper and a pen. If you prefer you can have a laptop computer. A lit candle is a universal beacon for all who are calling on the greater reality. After you've gone through the steps in Exercises 1 through 5, hold the intention of contacting the other side. Ask yourself: "Will I allow my intuition to work? Do I believe I can do this automatic writing and get results?" If you get any "No" answers, just keep practicing the exercises (1-6) until all the answers are "Yes." Then you will be able to move on to make contact in Exercise 7.

Step 7

Making initial contact: Know that you can accept or reject anything that comes through this process. Souls on the other side are in varying degrees of development, just like those on this side.

Then begin with: "Are you there?" Have a few more questions ready for your first encounter. Be prepared to write down anything that enters the clear, empty space in your mind. If a stray thought enters such as "This is not going to work," take a few breaths, empty your mind again and wait patiently. It is important to remember that you will not *hear* words. Channeling is a form of telepathy between two beings. There will be words as thought forms but no sounds. Write down whatever you receive. It's natural to be a little scared by trying this new activity. You will be fine. Your spirit guides are with you and you are protected. It's a new adventure.

The experience may last a few minutes or much longer. After the session is finished, see what was communicated.

~⊘

"Automatic Writing" or "Channeling"?

Sometimes a word is so heavy that you can use it as a doorstop. *Channeling* is such a word. Try dropping it into a casual conversation and chances are the word will bring it to a halt. Try saying, "I've been having conversations with my mother — channeling her on a regular basis" to a friend who knows your mother has been dead for 20 years. You learn very quickly how much taboo there is around mentioning contact with "the other side."

In order to encourage you, dear reader, to try your hand at contact, we use the less scary term, *automatic writing*. Many channeled books have been written through the techniques presented in this book, and authors sometimes use the terms *automatic writing* and *channeling* interchangeably.

Two excellent overview books also use both terms. The first is *Channeling: Investigations on Receiving Information from Paranormal Sources,* by parapsychologist Jon Klimo. The second is *With the Tongues of Men and Angels,* by psychologist and parapsychologist, Arthur Hastings. Here is Hastings' perspective:

[W]e find that channeling is natural in human experience and, even more, it has made desirable, positive contributions. Channeling is of service to humanity. It is a contact point between human personality and a source or sources that can be transcendent, wise, practical and inspirational. The study of channeling can remind us of this contact and can point to exceptional capabilities that are open to the human mind and heart.... It does not matter whether these potentials come from the personal unconscious of the individual, are brought about by a visiting outside entity, or draw on transpersonal levels of the self. They are there and one access to them is through the mental and physical processes of channeling.

You should also know that a few classic books refer to the practice of contacting people on the other side as *mediumship*. A medium is the term primarily used to describe a person who contacts a discarnate being on behalf of an incarnate person who wants that communication made through a psychic who demonstrates that ability. "Channeling" is also the term used to describe *trance channeling* — such as in the Jane Roberts/Seth books. Jane went into a semi-conscious trance and spoke the words of the discarnate entity Seth in a voice not her own. The words were recorded on paper or by tape recorder.

Channeling and *mediumship* can be scary words for many people. We want to give you fair warning that if you mention automatic writing, your listener will often mix that in with those other words. Again, for our purposes, Frances and I use the term *automatic writing*.

Deep Gratitude

Affairs are now soul size.
The enterprise
Is exploration into God.

These lines are contained in the Christopher Fry poem that opens Question 5: *What are we here to learn?* My gratitude extends to all those who are taking this step: to those who are ahead of us, to those who are co-creating it in their own ways, and most especially, to those who are taking this stride in consciousness with Frances and me. The "*Seven Questions Greater Reality* Series" is our attempt to add to the expansion of consciousness that seems so necessary to the survival of the human species.

It is true that we are spiritual beings first and foremost. And if you're reading this book, you are also having a human experience. Many of us who are incarnate at this moment recognize the need to put a larger frame on what's happening in order to address the existential crisis we face. We've been "exploring God" ever since our species looked up at the stars and thought a creator was up there somewhere. Now we're recognizing that we are fully participating co-creators in the All That Is. That's the next step.

So my boundless gratitude goes to my core group of mentors/supporters:

- Charles Garfield, my ever-present soulmate and teacher of compassion;
- Dan Drasin, my friend and mentor for 40 years, and teacher of the greater reality. He also took a final pass at the manuscript before design, and found the nit-pickiest things that needed attention;

- Regina Ochoa, whose gifts of mediumship and counseling keep me on track, and who keeps telling me how important these books are; and

- Judith Frank, dear friend, whose patient listening and feedback help ground me.

Seven Questions is blessed with a stellar production team:

- Naomi Rose is much more than an outstanding self-publishing consultant and editor. She also serves as an audience of one who raises questions about where the text might be vague or confusing to our readers. This spurs me to expand my own understanding to meet her challenge, since I don't change any of Frances's text.

- Margaret Copeland is the book's designer (both interior and cover). You can see for yourself what a fine work she's created here. And I bless her patience when I suggest changes that don't always work out.

- Gratitude to Gabriel Steinfeld who proofreads the back materials so meticulously and who loves commas. (As with *Book One*, any unconventional punctuation and grammar decisions are entirely made by the authors.)

- And to all the folks at Ingram/Spark, a division of Lightning Source print services, I say thank you for being on the team. And bringing the electronic version of the book into material reality.

To the people who read an early version of this book and pointed out bumps and foggy places in the parts I wrote, I am indebted to you for slogging through what needed improvement and for encouraging me to forge ahead: Shelli Fried, Patti Hamel, Elisabeth Belle, and Lura Dolas.

To Jon Klimo: After Frances and I completed *Seven Questions, Book One*, I was still wobbly from trying to navigate between the space/time world and "the other side." Your magnificent book, *Channeling*, provided me with the knowledge that I was in excellent company in a long lineage of people gifted with this ability. Your testimonial for Book Two is an honor. Thank you.

To Justine Willis Toms: You and I go way back to the early days of New Dimensions Radio and other groundbreaking organizations whose rallying cry was "A world that works for everyone." Here we are, still doing it, now with a broader vision. Thank you, dear friend, for your inspiration and support.

To Jeanne Love: Thank you for your ongoing enthusiastic support. You have channeled some of the best-known personalities of our time. Given your access to the greater reality, your testimonial is high praise. You meet with the souls on the other side of the veil as friends, allowing them their time with us, delivering their messages.

To Lisa Smartt: We met at a book signing where you spoke about *Veil*, the poetry book you channeled from your dad. I hadn't made a public appearance yet, and you gave me confidence that I could do it too. You have been a gift in my life. Thank you.

To our readers: Frances and I thank you for being with us every step of the way. From the vantage point of the greater reality, you informed us about what you needed to know, how to pace ourselves in presenting new material, how to *lighten* up (literally), and where to push the boundaries of consensus reality. This is your co-creation too.

And to you, Frances, I still marvel that you chose me to be your collaborator for *Book One*. Then for *Book Two* you showed up with more wisdom, more framing, more encouragement, especially when COVID-19 slowed the world down and made me think our book might arrive too late. Now I see how this unfolded for the best. This book answers for me, and I hope for our readers, such questions as: "What just happened? Was that an upheaval? What shall be the new normal? What expansion of consciousness did we gain that we don't want to lose?"

And to our precious planet, I want to deeply apologize for everything I have contributed to the destruction and loss of integrity of your sacred ecosystems and the extinction of other species. We are waking up to how the human systems we have co-created are not sustainable. The "current upheavals" are clear messages to us. As Frances has said, they also call forth incredible levels of heroic action and compassionate service from millions of people. But the costs of these lessons, in the forms of pain and grief, are very high. I'm hoping that the co-creation of *The Greater Reality* Series lights pathways to healing and visioning a more loving world. Thank you for your benevolent patience.

Permissions

Permission to quote from *The Intelligence of the Cosmos: Why Are We Here? New Answers from the Frontiers of Science* by Ervin Laszlo. Rochester, VT: Inner Traditions/Bear & Company, 2017. Received from publisher.

Permission to use the story of the Grateful Dead backstage pass, given by Justine Willis Toms, co-founder of New Dimensions Radio in 1973. New Dimensions has over 1500 radio programs archived as downloads or podcasts that feature a broad spectrum of thinkers on the leading edge of consciousness. See *www.newdimensions.org*

Permission to use segments from *Veil: Love Poems from Across the Threshold,* by Lisa Smartt and Morton Felix. University of Heaven, 2018. Given by Lisa Smartt.

About the Authors

Frances Vaughan was a psychologist and teacher who inspired everyone she met to be his or her higher self. She wrote books and papers that carried on the wisdom and compassion that she has gathered from many lifetimes. She served as a trustee for 19 years at the Fetzer Institute, which helps build a spiritual foundation for a loving world. As a transpersonal psychotherapist she helped guide her clients to find the source of their healing. She continues her work through this book collaboration.

"Frances was a respected 'Wise Woman' and a true elder. She embodied the strong feminine and was a model of an extraordinarily bright mind meeting an ever-expanding heart."

— Frank Osteseski, Founder of Metta Institute, author of
*The Five Invitations: Discovering What Death Can Teach Us
About Living Fully*

Books: *Awakening Intuition* (Anchor Books, 1979), *The Inward Arc: Healing in Psychotherapy and Spirituality* (iUniverse, 2001) and *Shadows of the Sacred: Seeing Through Spiritual Illusions* (Quest Books, 1995). With her husband, Roger Walsh, she was co-editor of *Paths Beyond Ego: The Transpersonal Vision* (Tarcher, 1993) and *Gifts from A Course in Miracles,* including *Accept this Gift, A Gift of Peace,* and *A Gift of Healing* (Tarcher, 1995), published separately and as one volume.

Cynthia Spring is an author, social activist, and explorer of the unconventional. Since the mid 1990s, she has been active in local ecology in the San Francisco area. She co-founded two ecology nonprofits, EarthTeam and Close to Home, as well as serving as coordinator for Earth Day 2000 for the Bay Area. Her explorations have been in the fields of spirituality, transpersonal psychology and personal growth. She lives in Northern California with her husband Charlie, and two cats, Bella and Layla.

Books: *Seven Questions About Life After Life*, in collaboration with Frances Vaughan (Wisdom Circles Publishing, 2019); *The Wave and The Drop: Wisdom Stories about Death and Afterlife* (Wisdom Circles Publishing, 2018), *Wisdom Circles: A Guide to Self-Discovery and Community Building in Small Groups* (Hyperion, 1998). She co-authored *Sometimes My Heart Goes Numb: Love and Caregiving in a Time of AIDS* with Charles Garfield (Jossey-Bass 1995). She co-edited the anthology *Earthlight: Spiritual Wisdom for an Ecological Age* (2007). She was also the producer (1981-1996) of over 100 nonfiction audiobooks. See *https://cindyspring.com*.

Lightning Source UK Ltd.
Milton Keynes UK
UKHW041236130921
390500UK00003B/478